Praise for *Risk-Return Analysis*

"Harry Markowitz invented portfolio analysis and presented the theory in his famous 1952 article and 1959 book. Sixty-one years after his initial work, he is writing a four-volume series of books based on his continued development of portfolio theory and management. Nobody has greater insight into the process than Harry. In this first volume, he describes with great clarity and insight rational decision making and the key role of mean-variance analysis. Harry not only answers any questions that have been raised, but also some that haven't been thought of. No academic or practitioner can truly claim to understand portfolio analysis unless they have read this volume. I eagerly await volumes 2, 3, and 4 as Harry continues to educate us all."
—**Martin J. Gruber**, Professor Emeritus and Scholar in Residence of the Stern School of Business, New York University

"How to use available historical data to quantify the rewards to long-term investing is one of the most important problems in finance. Surveying the vast literature inspired by his own 1959 book, *Portfolio Selection: Efficient Diversification of Investments,* has stimulated an outpouring of ideas. He builds on the strengths and limitations of the important papers in order to come up with a position that should silence a lot of critics."
—**Jack Treynor**, President of Treynor Capital Management

"Most people praise the Modern Portfolio Theory (MPT) paradigm innovated by Nobel Laureate Harry Markowitz, and a few people criticize it, but all share one thing in common: they use it intensively in their academic research and in practical investments alike. What makes the MPT so immense is the amazing optimal combination of three elements: a profound analytical base, strong intuition and a simplicity that makes it easy to implement. No wonder it is still a pillar of modern finance even after six decades since its publication, and I have no doubt it will be the center of modern finance theory for many more years to come. Volume 1 in the series thoroughly covers important investment topics and their relation to the MPT, emphasizing that the mean-variance rule can serve as an excellent approximation to expected utility in virtually all investment scenarios. The authors do not overlook various criticisms of the MPT, but rather address them convincingly. This excellent book is an essential reference to academics and practitioners alike."
—**Haim Levy**, Dean of the School of Business, Hebrew University, Jerusalem, Israel

Harry Markowitz's ground-breaking 1952 and 1959 publications on Portfolio Selection prescribe a methodology that a rational decision-maker can follow to optimize his investment portfolio in a risky world. *Risk-Return Analysis* is the first installment of a four-part opus that critically reviews and summarizes the academic work on modern portfolio theory that Harry and others have published during the six decades that have followed. This challenging new book clarifies many common misconceptions about modern portfolio theory. It is a wonderful gift to the investment profession.

—**Roger C. Gibson**, Author, *Asset Allocation: Balancing Financial Risk*, Chief Investment Officer, Gibson Capital, LLC

"One hundred years from now, students of financial economics will begin their training by learning mean-variance analysis and portfolio optimization, thanks to the pioneering work of Harry Markowitz. Few scholars have had such impact on both theory and practice as Markowitz, and these volumes contain great wisdom that every economist, portfolio manager, and investor should savor page by page."

—**Andrew W. Lo, Charles E. and Susan T. Harris**, Professor and Director, Laboratory for Financial Engineering MIT Sloan School of Management

"Harry Markowitz is a force of nature in our field. He is like a seasonal cyclone that tears through the city of received knowledge and rearranges all the conceptual buildings—invariably for the better.

His monumental work in the 1950s would be sufficient to qualify as a lifetime achievement for most mortals, but he keeps spouting fresh insights like lightning flashes year after year, and penetrating ever deeper into the theory, mathematics and practice of investing.

Harry Markowitz is without parallel in his intellectual honesty, his enthusiasm, and his courage to tackle the biggest intellectual challenges. He exhibits a compulsion to probe ever deeper into the fundamental mysteries of finance, even when the new findings lead to refining or even upending some of his own prior work. You would think he would occasionally take a breather, give it a brief respite, a pause—if only to allow the rest of us to catch up—but no, Markowitz is relentless in his intellectual pursuit to develop a more comprehensive understanding of all aspects of the investment process.

The current volume, *Risk-Return Analysis*, integrates a cornucopia of Markowitz's latest thinking, together with the author's structural overview of the current state of the field. The subtitle, *The Theory and Practice of Rational Investing*, really speaks to two goals. With respect to the first goal, Markowitz and Blay do indeed succeed in presenting a comprehensive theory of investing that is fresh, coherent, authoritative, and yet readable. With the second, and much more challenging goal of injecting rationality into the practice of investing, this book will at least help move the reader a long way down the right path.

—**Martin Leibowitz**, Managing Director, Global Research Strategy, Morgan Stanley

Risk-Return Analysis

RISK-RETURN ANALYSIS

The Theory and Practice of Rational Investing

Volume I

HARRY M. MARKOWITZ

WITH **KENNETH A. BLAY**

New York   Chicago   San Francisco   Athens   London   Madrid
Mexico City   Milan   New Delhi   Singapore   Sydney   Toronto

Copyright © 2014 by Harry M. Markowitz and Kenneth A. Blay. All rights reserved. Printed in the United States of America. Except as permitted under the United States Copyright Act of 1976, no part of this publication may be reproduced or distributed in any form or by any means, or stored in a data base or retrieval system, without prior written permission of the publisher.

1 2 3 4 5 6 7 8 9 0   DOC/DOC   1 9 8 7 6 5 4 3

ISBN: 978-0-07-181793-6
MHID: 0-07-181793-X

e-ISBN: 978-0-07-181794-3
e-MHID: 0-07-181794-8

McGraw-Hill books are available at special quantity discounts to use as premiums and sales promotions, or for use in corporate training programs. To contact a representative, please visit the Contact Us page at www.mhprofessional.com.

This book is printed on acid-free paper.

DEDICATION

Barbara (Mrs. Markowitz) and I were each married twice before. She brought two children to our marriage from one of her prior marriages; I brought four from two of my prior marriages. Having dedicated a previous book to Barbara, I would like to dedicate the current one to

Our children
(in order of appearance in the world):

David, Sue, Jim, Fred, Laurie, and Steven,

And to our grandchildren
(organized by family groups)

Becky, Michalina, Ben, and Lee; Melody,
Brenden, and Amy; Helen; Lauren, and Chris; Rashayna,
(a different) Lauren, and Mick;

And to our great-grandchildren Merle;
Cyrus and Elijah; Miles; Henry and Molly;
(one on the way); Collin, Kieran,
and Finn; Malachi and Zoe; Jaden, Dasan, and Ryder

Barbara and I were only children.

Kenneth Blay
  To my parents, George and Mirta, and my wife, Viviana

CONTENTS

Foreword	xi
Preface	xxi
Acknowledgments	xxvii
Outline of Plans for Volumes II, III, and IV	xxix
1. The Expected Utility Maxim	**1**
Introduction	1
Definitions	5
Uniqueness	10
Characteristics of Expected Utility Maximization	12
RDMs Versus HDMs	14
Allais's Paradox	17
Weber's Law and the Allais Paradox	21
The Axioms	24
Axiom I	25
Axiom II	26
Axioms III and III'	28
Bounded Versus Unbounded Utility of Returns	31
Postscript	34

viii • Contents

2. Mean-Variance Approximations to Expected Utility — 37
Introduction — 37
Why Not Just Maximize Expected Utility? — 41
Utility of Return Versus Utility of Wealth — 44
Loistl's Erroneous Analysis — 47
Levy and Markowitz (1979) — 48
Highly Risk-Averse Investors — 53
Highly Risk-Averse Investors and a Risk-Free Asset — 56
Portfolios of Call Options — 58
Ederington's Quadratic and Gaussian Approximations to Expected Utility — 63
Other Pioneers — 69
Conclusion — 72

3. Mean-Variance Approximations to the Geometric Mean — 73
Introduction — 73
Why Inputs to a Mean-Variance Analysis Must Be Arithmetic Means — 78
Six Mean-Variance Approximations to g — 80
Observed Approximation Errors for Asset Classes — 84
Relationships Among Approximation Methods — 90
Twentieth-Century Real Equity Returns — 97
Choice of Approximation — 111
Recap — 117
Technical Note: Selecting a Weighted Average of Approximations — 118

4. Alternative Measures of Risk — 123
Introduction — 123
The Asset-Class Database — 124
Comparisons — 127
The DMS Database — 137
Caveat and Conclusion — 147

5. The Likelihood of Various Return Distributions (*With Anthony Tessitore, Ansel Tessitore, and Nilufer Usmen*) — 149
Introduction — 149
Bayes Factors — 153
Transformed Variables — 156
Compound Hypotheses — 159
The Pearson Family — 161
The DMS Database — 169
Practically Normal Distributions — 175
Illustrative Histograms — 179
Near LH-Maximizing Distributions for the Ensemble — 182
Transformed Country Distributions — 186
Observations — 190
Recommendation — 192

Notes — 195

References — 209

Index — 217

FOREWORD

The process of selecting a portfolio may be divided into two stages. The first stage starts with observation and experience and ends with beliefs about the future performances of available securities. The second stage starts with the relevant beliefs about future performances and ends with the choice of portfolio. This paper is concerned with the second stage.

—Harry M. Markowitz (1952)

It was Markowitz who first made risk the centerpiece of portfolio management by focusing on what investing is all about: investing is a bet on an unknown future. ... Markowitz's famous comment that "you think about risk as well as return" sounds like a homey slogan today. Yet it was a total novelty in 1952 to give risk at least equal weight in the search for reward. Nothing more deeply divide[s] [modern finance] from the world before 1952.

—Peter Bernstein (2007)

[F]rom the very beginning of modern finance—from our big bang, as it were—which I think we can all agree today dates to the year 1952 with the publication in

> *the Journal of Finance of Harry Markowitz's article, "Portfolio Selection" ...*
> —Merton Miller (2000)

> *Markowitz came along, and there was light.*
> —William F. Sharpe, quoted in Bernstein (2007)

The ideas that Harry Markowitz published more than 60 years ago have become the foundation on which thousands of future academics, scholars, and practitioners anchored their own worldviews. His ideas now serve as the stimulative energy for countless efforts to further perfect the science of diversified portfolio construction and even bolder attempts to create entirely new portfolio science narratives.

Early in my portfolio management career, my reading of Brinson, Hood, and Beebower's 1986 study of asset allocation of 91 pension funds triggered my appreciation for mean and variance as the very best supportable and sustainable framework for portfolio construction. I immersed myself in what is now widely and only fairly recently known as Modern Portfolio Theory, or MPT.

Although I am a Chartered Financial Analyst charterholder and a Certified Public Accountant, I am not a trained academic, I am a businessman. However, I live comfortably in both the academic and the business communities. To my academic friends, I am a businessman who respects excellent scholarly work and willingly and frequently provides financial benevolence toward both primary and practical research.

To my business friends, I am an intensely focused teacher who can get lost in the nuanced weeds of exploring and explaining ideas that matter. Regrettably, I see far too much intellectual laziness, even intellectual dishonesty, in both academia and the business world.

The purpose of business is to make people's lives better. Period. I am a disciplined student and practitioner of portfolio management sciences. The investment firm I lead takes the responsibility of managing billions of dollars of portfolio value for hundreds of thousands of clients very seriously. Their future happiness depends in large part on us. As a duty and a discipline, we seek truth as a guiding principle. We are fully prepared for the journey on which truth seeking takes us, even if it puts us uncomfortably on the defensive. Being right and good is far more important than being successful and prosperous. It is better to be admired for virtue than envied for success. But I believe there does not have to be any incompatibility between the two ideals. It is liberating to know that being right and being successful are not mutually exclusive.

As for most investment practitioners, the gravity of the responsibility I have is heavy. My firm and I continuously examine and monitor the evolution of new paradigms and new blasphemous challenges to our worldview. As stewards of other people's assets, it is our duty to do so.

In the 1980s, as a young investment analyst and portfolio manager for a small securities broker-dealer, my primary responsibility was to research and design model asset allocation portfolios. I became engrossed by the philosophical and practical logic of mean-variance analysis. It was a process that simply made sense, but I rapidly saw that good judgment was essential for achieving its benefits and that the use of mindless heuristics, general rules of thumb, and shallow reasoning would inevitably cause some practitioners to feel betrayed by it.

I developed a reverent appreciation for many things MPT, especially the sensitivity of the efficient frontier to very small changes in inputs of expected returns, variances, and correlation estimates. The earliest days of the DOS-based personal computers facilitated quick calculations of thousands of iterations of efficient frontiers, which enabled an appreciation of the idea that small changes in input assumptions can create huge variations in portfolio design. Just as physical sports practice leads to muscle memory in a world-class athlete, this repetitive process resulted in a refinement of judgment, a keen sensitivity to risk, and an appreciation for nuance in portfolio construction. Put another way, an obvious benefit of this intensely focused exercise was a highly developed intuition about the utilitarian trade-offs when seeking higher returns and targeted terminable values.

Good judgment and practical wisdom cannot be overemphasized as essential factors for success, and these virtues are born in large part from a serious, nonsuperficial study of the history of capital markets. Modern Portfolio Theory is based on probability beliefs about the future, not directly on a replication of objective probabilities derived from the past, although the past is an important teacher. The curse of intellectual laziness has, in my opinion, caused some of the hostile and unfounded commentary about MPT. Understanding fully how we formulate beliefs about the future is paramount for success in the practical use of MPT. Being consummately self-aware of Bayes' rule and the stream of conditional probabilities in which we must navigate is a necessary discipline for any MPT practitioner's success.

The financial collapse of 2008 and 2009 resulted in a tremendous and sudden decline in worldwide wealth as correlations between most asset pairs coalesced toward one. The tsunami created from the perfect storm of misunderstood, underappreciated, underpriced, and unknown systemic risks in the U.S. housing market, collateralized mortgage obligations, easy Fed monetary policy, the securitization of mortgage debt around the world, $600 trillion of derivative instrument counterparty exposure, excess portfolio leverage, and the sudden absence of liquidity temporarily overwhelmed the diversification benefits of asset allocation. This trauma precipitated a serious questioning of the efficacy of MPT diversified portfolios. People wondered whether we had entered a new era, with a need for new rules of portfolio construction and a new understanding of risk that trumped the conventional ideas of systemic and idiosyncratic risk. Like many practitioners, my colleagues and I began wondering whether the MPT paradigm had run its course. To borrow the lyrics from a popular song by the group R.E.M., I was possibly "Losing My Religion" about MPT. Was it time to be a courageous Bayesian? To learn from the evidence, update our probability beliefs, abandon the paradigm that got us where we were, and move on?

We contacted Harry to obtain answers to our new questions about MPT. We owed it to our clients and our affiliated professional financial advisors to do so. Harry accepted our invitation to be a consultant and advisor to our firm's investment committee. That initial phone call was the beginning of a meaningful business partnership that has since evolved into a warm and important friendship. As a beneficial consequence of our professional affiliation and personal friendship, we are today, more than ever, vociferous and enthusiastic advocates of MPT. We are motivated financial and research benefactors to Harry Markowitz in the production and publishing of the multiple volumes of this book.

One example of the numerous benefits derived from our partnership was his response to our first and urgent question regarding whether MPT necessarily assumed that asset-class return distributions are Gaussian. We felt that somehow the capital markets crisis introduced extreme long-tail events, extreme skewness and kurtosis, and thus nonnormality in asset-class distributions that negated the usefulness of MPT. My specific question to Harry was, "Does MPT work in a nonnormal world?" For the answer to that question, in our very first consultation, Harry calmly directed us to Table 2 on page 121 of his seminal 1959 textbook, *Portfolio Selection*, and showed us proof that, from the very beginning, MPT never assumed or required a normal distribution, and that MPT works soundly in nonnormal worlds. In addition, he confidently showed that equity performance in 2008 and 2009 was not a long-tail event, but actually fit within a little over two standard deviations of historical mean returns. Although what happened in 2008 and 2009 was painful, there was nothing that occurred then that was unusual or outside of our peripheral vision. "Wow!" was all we could say in response, with tremendous relief. Harry had pondered this very issue, as he had so many others, at least 50 years ago! He wrote in a journal in 2010 that "while writing my 1959 book ... I concluded that, for many utility functions, if probability distributions are not too spread out, then a quadratic approximation fits quite well. In that case the mean-variance approximation to expected utility is quite good—*no matter what shape of the distribution!*" [emphasis added]

With Harry's assistance, we examined the foundations of our own beliefs encased in our model asset allocation portfolios. With great relief, we confirmed that our prior beliefs and assumptions were still relevant and accordingly made only small changes to our portfolios.

Our curiosity increased about our understanding of the entire framework of MPT. We wondered whether, if we, as longtime practitioners and advocates, did not understand the basic premise of return distribution "nonnormality," were there other premises that we were probably misunderstanding? If I and my firm were confused about some important elements of MPT, then how many other practitioners and academics were confused? The answer, I am sure, is probably hundreds of thousands.

We felt the whole portfolio management world would soon begin asking the same questions about MPT. It did. Predictably, the early concerns morphed into outright attacks on MPT in academic and practitioner journals from 2009 through 2012. "MPT had failed us. Diversification does not work. What went wrong with MPT?" they all exclaimed in chorus. Since then, Harry Markowitz has officially and aptly labeled this period "the Great Confusion," to which this writing is the beginning of a multivolume remedy and hopefully a permanent antidote.

Our research partnership and consultation has been very gratifying and many times electrifying. In addition to asset return nonnormality, some of the many other questions we had about MPT included the efficacy of the various methods for approximating geometric returns using only mean and variance, decision making over multiple periods given known and unknown odds, alternative approaches to creating efficient frontiers, optimal portfolio rebalancing protocols, alternatives to variance as a definition of risk (we considered alternatives such as semivariance, value at risk, and conditional value at risk), the effects of leverage and significant illiquidity on MPT efficient frontiers, the effect of incorporating a tax-averse rational investor into the MPT framework and how to create tax-cognizant efficient frontiers, and the validity of the premise of the rational decision maker within the new field of behavioral finance. For 60 years, an abundance of scholarly work related to aspects of MPT has been performed. It seemed that the Great Confusion was the catalyst for systematically revisiting much of this research.

For Harry to respond to these new and old questions, I am reminded of the ancient craft of apologetics from Greek antiquity. To deliver an *apologia* meant making a formal speech or giving an explanation replying to and defending against heresy or challenges to a particular philosophical or religious doctrine. Apologetics wrongly implies a modern notion of apology, for which MPT requires none. Harry succinctly states that his ideas in his 1952 essay and 1959 book *Portfolio Selection* were a priori. Now, after 61 years of practice, analysis, and research, the systematic and reasoned writings in these volumes will firmly demonstrate that Harry Markowitz's ideas in *Portfolio Selection* have provided the world with a far better investment process than what he ever imagined in 1952! The Great Confusion will become "the Deep Understanding," and we all will be better for it.

Stephen A. Batman
CEO and Founder
1st Global, Inc.
March 1, 2013

REFERENCES

Bernstein, P. (2007). *Capital Ideas Evolving.* Hoboken, NJ: John Wiley & Sons, pp. xii–xiii.

Markowitz, H. M. (1952). "Portfolio Selection." *Journal of Finance* 7(1):77–91.

———— (1959). *Portfolio Selection: Efficient Diversification of Investments*, 2nd ed. New York: John Wiley & Sons; 2nd ed. Cambridge, MA: Basil Blackwell, 1991.

Miller. M. H. (2000). "The History of Finance: An Eyewitness Account." *Journal of Applied Corporate Finance* 13:8–14.

PREFACE

The present volume presents Part I of a planned four-part book on the theory and practice of risk-return analysis, particularly mean-variance analysis. This field is plagued by a Great Confusion, namely the confusion between necessary and sufficient conditions for the use of mean-variance analysis in practice. Normal (Gaussian) return distributions are sufficient to justify the use of mean-variance analysis, but they are not necessary. If you believe (as many do, including the undersigned) that rational decision making should be consistent with expected utility maximization, then the necessary and sufficient condition for the use of mean-variance analysis in practice is that a carefully selected portfolio from a mean-variance efficient set will approximately maximize expected utility for a wide variety of concave (risk-averse) utility functions. This was the argument for mean-variance analysis I presented in Markowitz (1959).

The first of the following two sections of this preface briefly reviews the fundamental assumptions of Markowitz (1959), of which the maximization of single-period expected utility is a part. The second section relates these fundamental assumptions to the contents of the present book, including the present volume and the plans for Parts II, III, and IV.

MARKOWITZ'S FUNDAMENTAL ASSUMPTIONS

Markowitz (1959) justifies mean-variance analysis by relating it to the theory of rational decision making over time and under uncertainty as developed by von Neumann and Morgenstern (1944), L. J. Savage (1954), and R. Bellman (1957). The fundamental assumptions of the book appear in Part IV, Chapters 10 through 13. Specifically,

- Chapter 10 deals with single-period decision making with known odds. It echoes the view that, in this case, the rational decision maker (RDM) may be assumed to follow certain axioms, from which follows the expected utility maxim.
- Chapter 11 of Markowitz (1959) considers many-period games, still with known odds. It shows that essentially the same set of axioms as in Chapter 10 implies that an RDM would maximize expected utility for the game as a whole, which, in turn, implies that the RDM would maximize the expected values of a sequence of *single-period* utility functions, each using a Bellman "derived" utility function.
- Chapter 12 of Markowitz (1959) considers single- or multiple-period decision making with unknown odds. Based on Savage's work, it adds a "sure thing" principle to the axioms of Chapters 10 and 11 and concludes that when odds are unknown, the RDM maximizes expected utility using "probability beliefs" where

objective probabilities are not known. As evidence accumulates, these probability beliefs shift according to Bayes' rule.

- Chapter 13 applies the conclusions of Chapters 10 through 12 to the portfolio selection problem. In particular, it extends to other utility functions an observation made in Chapter 6 for logarithmic utility: that if the probability distribution of a portfolio's returns is not "too spread out," a function of its mean and variance closely approximates its expected utility.

The reason these fundamental assumptions appeared at the back of the book rather than at the front was that I feared that if I started with an axiomatic treatment of the theory of rational decision making under uncertainty, no one involved with managing money would read the book. This may have been a good strategy at the time, but its side effect is that only a very small percentage of our industry understands the conditions for the applicability of mean-variance analysis.

OUTLINE OF CURRENT BOOK

It is planned that the current book will have four parts. At the suggestion of Frank Fabozzi, each part will be published separately when completed.

Markowitz (1959) may be thought of as having three major aspects. One aspect is the theoretical justification for the use of mean-variance analysis. As noted earlier, this appears mostly in Part IV of that book. A second aspect of Markowitz (1959) is computational. In particular, the critical line algorithm for tracing out mean-variance efficient frontiers is illustrated geometrically in Chapter 7 numerically in Chapter 8, and its correctness is demonstrated in Appendix A. The third aspect of Markowitz (1959) is a catchall that includes an exposition of the basic concepts of portfolio mean and variance and how these relate to the means, variances, and covariances of individual securities, plus special topics such as the "law of the average covariance" in Chapter 5 and the semivariance, now known as downside risk, in Chapter 9.

Markowitz (1987), later reissued as Markowitz and Todd (2000), was a more thorough exposition of the computational aspects than was presented in Markowitz (1959). The present book similarly is a more thorough discussion of the fundamental assumptions behind mean-variance analysis than I presented in Part IV of Markowitz (1959). In particular:

- Part I of the current book—like Chapter 10 in Markowitz (1959)—is concerned with the theory of rational decision making for single-period decision situations with known odds. It focuses on mean-variance approximations to expected utility, including a chapter that surveys the research on this subject from 1959 to the present and two chapters that extend such research.

Preface • xxv

- Part II of this book, like Chapter 11 of Markowitz (1959), will be concerned with rational decision making for the many-period game and its relationship to single-period utility maximization, still assuming known odds. It will include topics such as Jan Mossin's myopic utility, the Markowitz and van Dijk (2003) heuristic for approximating the Bellman derived utility function in high-dimensional state spaces, and the Blay and Markowitz analysis of tax-cognizant asset allocation.

- Part III of the current book, like Chapter 12 of Markowitz (1959), is concerned with single- or many-period games with unknown odds. It is planned to include a discussion of Richard Michaud's (1998) resampling and the Black-Litterman (1991) procedure as these relate to the Bayesian view recommended in Markowitz (1959).

- Part IV of the current book differs in purpose from Chapter 13 of Markowitz (1959). The latter, titled "Applications to Portfolio Selection," was concerned with the practical application of the theory presented in the three chapters that preceded it. In the present book, such applications are presented along with the theory in Parts I, II, and III themselves. Part IV of the present book is concerned with additional application issues not addressed in the earlier parts of the book, especially the division of labor among data, theory, computation, and the human. In this connection, the human enters as both producer and consumer of portfolio analysis.

This is clearly an ambitious program, especially considering that the undersigned is in his mid-eighties. Following this preface and acknowldgements is an outline of plans for Parts II, III, and IV. The aim is to provide enough information so that a diligent scholar could more or less reproduce these parts as now planned in the event that the undersigned is unable to do so.

Harry Markowitz
San Diego, CA
March 1, 2013

ACKNOWLEDGMENTS

This book has been sponsored by 1st Global of Dallas, Texas. I would like to thank 1st Global in general, and in particular I am delighted to thank Steven Anthony (Tony) Batman, the CEO of 1st Global, and David Knoch, its president. Kenneth Blay has been my chief contact with 1st Global on this and other matters. In particular, we have worked together on certain issues, such as tax-cognizant investment (to be discussed in Part II of this book). Given our close and continuing relationship in the production of this book, it seemed to me that the appropriate acknowledgement for Ken Blay was to list him as a joint author.

This book reflects 60 years of discussions and observations regarding the theory and practice of risk-return analysis. Over the years, I have benefited much from repeated discussions on various aspects of this topic, especially with Jack Francis, Roger Gibson, Marty Gruber, John Guerard, Mark Kritzman, Haim Levy, Richard and Robert Michaud, Bill Sharpe (who started as my student and since has often been my teacher), Sam Savage, Tony Tessitore, Peter Todd, Jack Treynor, Steve Turi, Nilufer Usmen, Ming Yee Wang, and Gan

Lin Xu. More recently or less frequently, but nevertheless of great value to me, have been discussions with the following:

Tom Anachini	Lisa Goldberg	Ana Marjanski
Rob Arnott	Sherrie Grabot	Bob Merton
Joseph Blasi	Gil Hammer	André Perold
Marian Bloch	Mark Hebner	Alex Potts
Marshall Blume	Bruce Jacobs	Don Reid
Mary Brunson	Sharan Jagpal	Mark Rubinstein
Joni Clark	Paul Kaplan	
Kane Cotton	Krzysztof (Christoff) Kontek	Sam Savage
Sanjiv Das		Jonathan Scheid
Erik van Dijk	Marty Leibowitz	Yusif Simaan
Ned Elton	Ken Levy	Bob Sullivan
Frank Fabozzi	Andy Lo	Bernie Tew
Gifford Fong	Mark Machina	Bill Ziemba

and countless students, teaching assistants, luncheon guests, colleagues in other fields, and, in memorium, Peter Bernstein, Larry Fisher, and Paul Samuelson. Finally, I am more than delighted to thank my secretary, Mary (Midge) McDonald, for her patience in typing innumerable drafts of this volume, and my wife, Barbara, who helped make it all fun.

OUTLINE OF PLANS FOR VOLUMES II, III, AND IV

VOLUME II

Volume II is planned to present the following ideas in roughly the following order:

- The concept of a game in the sense of von Neumann and Morgenstern, and especially their concept of a *strategy*—namely, a rule that specifies a player's move in every circumstance in which the player may find itself.

On questions of asset allocation we will principally be concerned with single-person games. Two-person and n-person games can be relevant to questions of trading strategies, on which we will say little if anything.

- The notion of utility attached to the game as a whole as presented in Markowitz (1959), Chapter 11 with emphasis here, as there, on the fact that such a utility function is *not necessarily a separable function* of single-period utilities.

We will illustrate this point in terms of a utility function:

$$U = U(C_1, C_2, \ldots, C_t, W_{T+1}) \qquad (1)$$

where C_t is consumption expenditures in year t, W_{T+1} is bequest level and U reflects the negative impact of *declines* in consumption as well as a present value of the C_t stream.

- The axiomatic justification for maximizing the expected utility of the game-as-a-whole is presented in Markowitz (1959), Chapter 11.
- Dynamic programming's backward recursive method of solving many-period games as presented in Bellman (1957); especially how dynamic programming reduces the many-period game to a *sequence of single-period expected utility maximizations*.

Mossin's (1968) analysis of myopic utility functions will serve to illustrate dynamic programming for a highly simplified investment game. We will interpret Markowitz (1952b) with its utility analysis of *deviations* from current wealth, $\triangle W_t$—as distinguished from the level of end-of-period wealth, W_{t+1}—as a Bellman "derived" utility function when U in Equation 1 reflects the disutility (so to speak) of declines in consumption:

- The observation in Markowitz (1959) Chapter 11, the section on "Intermediate Decision, Incomplete Outcomes," that a utility analysis may apply to "the game as a whole" but not for the choice of portfolio separately; versus the observation in Markowitz (1959) Chapter 13—spelled out in greater detail in "the game of life" in Markowitz (1991)—that a realistic consumption-investment game is orders of magnitude more complex than can be solved in a human lifetime.

In particular, decisions as to how much to save or withdraw this period, or how cautiously to invest this period, depend on status and events involving education, employment, housing, car(s) and other durable goods, marriages, births, health, etc. This is the rationale for:

- The divisions of labor between the human and the computer proposed in Markowitz (1959), Chapter 13, starting with a "plain vanilla" division of labor where the computer's only job is to present the human with a menu of "good" probability distributions of return on the portfolio-as-a-whole for a forthcoming interval of time.

This leaves it to the human to make complex decisions as to how much to reserve for consumption expenditures during the period, how much to spend on either consumer durables or illiquid investments, etc. Information concerning available portfolio return distributions may influence such choices:

- Other Markowitz (1959) Chapter 13 suggestions for mean-variance analysis when the implicit dynamic program has state-variables other than end-of-period wealth.

In particular, since covariance between portfolio return and another state-variable (e.g., inflation) is linear in investment weights, it can be introduced as a linear constraint in the portfolio selection model:

- Tracking-error versus total variability. Also, variance of asset value minus the present value of liabilities as in Sharpe and Tint (1990).

The complexity of a dynamic programming calculation depends primarily on the number of states the game can enter. This in turn typically depends on the number of *state-variables* which describe the state, and the range of values which these can take on. For example, Sun, et al. (2006) describe a portfolio rebalancing problem with five state-variables, namely, the deviations from optimal of five stocks to be rebalanced. Using a grid with 15 points in each of the five dimensions of the state-space, this five-security problem pushed the limits of the then available super-computer capabilities:

- Markowitz and van Dijk (2003) provides a "quadratic surrogate" method for approximately optimizing a high-dimensional dynamic game.

The Markowitz and van Dijk heuristic proved to be quite good, both in the solvable sample problem in the Markowitz and van Dijk article, and on the afore mentioned five-security rebalancing problem as reported by Kritzman, Myrgren, and Page (2009). The method scales up to very high-dimensional systems, and is being used in fact to rebalance large institutional portfolios.

The following is an alternate approach to certain high-dimensional many-period games for which the Markowitz-van Dijk heuristic is not applicable:

- The Blay-Markowitz mean-variance analysis of the Net Present Value (NPV) of asset classes in accounts with different tax status, e.g., large-cap stocks in a taxable account versus large-cap stocks in tax-deferred accounts.

PART III

Part III will incorporate the following ideas:

- Philosophical background, especially Descartes (1968, originally published in 1641), Hume (1955, originally published in 1748), and L. J. Savage (1964).

Each in its own way, the first two show that no empirical hypothesis can be proved with certainty. Savage resolves the quandary in which the first two leave us by asserting, in effect, that we should not try to answer, *"What do we know?"* but should seek rather, *"How should we act?"*

- Formalization of the decision under uncertainty problem (with m possible outcomes and n possible hypotheses about the world, where m and n may be astronomical in size) as in Markowitz (1959), Chapter 12, namely, as that of choosing among "strategy matrices" P, Q, R, e.g.:

$$P = (p_{ij})$$

where p_{ij} is the probability of the *i-th* outcome if hypothesis *j* is true and the strategy represented by matrix *P* is followed.

- The expected utility rule using probability beliefs (*EU / PB*)
- Bayes rule.
- The Markowitz (1959), Chapter 12 axioms for *EU / PB*.

These are the same as the axioms for *EU* in Parts I and II, plus a *sure thing* axiom.

- The RDM versus the HDM. Time consistency. The Ellsberg (1961) objection and response.
- The Hildreth (1963) view of the Bayesian statistician serving Bayesian *remote clients.*

The Hildreth view is contrasted with the use of conjugate priors:

- Bayesian versus Neyman-Pearson inference (Markowitz and Usmen 1996a and b). Lindley's paradox.
- Resampled frontiers versus Bayesian inference. (Michaud 1998, Markowitz and Usmen 2003).

- Black and Litterman (1991).
- A Bayesian view of robust statistical inference.

PART IV

For the most part, Part IV will review standard practice with respect to various implementation topics. Current plans include the following topics:

- Basic decisions with respect to the universe of securities or asset classes, frequency of reoptimization, rebalancing and benchmarks if any.
- The roles of portfolio constraints.
- Related technical topics including rebalancing and "volatility capture."
- Sensitivity of optimality to round-off.
- Monte Carlo tests of policies and data mining. (Markowitz and Xu 1994).
- Top-down analysis starting at an asset class level. (Brinson et al. 1986 and 1991).
- Data "versus" judgment in forward looking estimates, e.g., Arnott and Bernstein (2002).

More generally, there will be a discussion of ways of combining data and judgment in parameter estimates:

- Statistical estimates from series of different length.
- Efficient-portfolio confidence intervals.
- Can money managers beat their benchmarks?

It is at least as important for the financial advisor to help his or her client invest at the *appropriate part* of the efficient frontier—appropriate for the specific client, of course—as it is to be on or near the frontier. The following are ways in which this is approached:

- Questionnaires.
- "Buckets" or "mental accounts."
- Monte Carlo analysis.

The last of these can also help evaluate (1) whether the client's planned savings rate is likely to prove adequate for the client's retirement needs, and (2) the consequences of spending rates and annuity decisions during retirement.

Finally, we should attempt a look to the future—namely, how could portfolio analysis take advantage of greatly increased computing and communication speeds, data storage and access capabilities, and data availability.

- Will a human-devised algorithm ever again create radically new hypotheses, as Einstein did more than once in 1905?
- How not to drown in exabytes of data.

This raises questions of how to organize data, hypotheses, analysts' forecasts, predictions versus actuals, etc.

- In the limit we approach the RDM—for whom the lessons of Descartes and Hume still hold.

1

THE EXPECTED UTILITY MAXIM

INTRODUCTION

As explained in the preceding preface to the four parts planned for the present book, the fundamental assumptions of Markowitz (1959) are in its Part 4, Chapters 10 through 13. These fundamental assumptions are at the back rather than the front of Markowitz (1959) because Markowitz feared that no practitioner would read a book that began with an axiomatic treatment of the theory of rational decision making under uncertainty. But now, clearly, these matters have become urgent. They bear directly on controversies such as:

- Under what conditions one should use mean-variance (MV) analysis
- What should be used in its stead when mean-variance analysis is not applicable

- How a single-period risk-return analysis relates to its many-period context
- How parameter uncertainty should be handled

It may seem frivolous to carefully weigh questions such as:

If an investor prefers Portfolio A to Portfolio B, should that investor prefer to go with Portfolio A, or would it be as good or better to toss a coin to choose between Portfolio A and Portfolio B?

Or again, if the investor prefers Portfolio A to Portfolio B, should he or she prefer Portfolio B for sure or a 50-50 chance of A or B?

Perhaps surprisingly, the answers to such questions imply how one should judge alternative measures of risk.

For example, two measures of risk that have been proposed are (1) standard deviation and (2) maximum loss. But maximum loss is a risk measure that violates the principle that if one prefers Portfolio A to Portfolio B, one should prefer a chance of Portfolio A to the certainty of Portfolio B. For example, suppose that Portfolio A has a 50-50 chance of a 30 percent gain or a 10 percent loss, whereas Portfolio B has a 50-50 chance of a 40 percent gain or a 20 percent loss. Both have an expected (a.k.a. average or "mean") return of 10 percent. Portfolio A has a standard deviation of 20 percent and a maximum loss of 10 percent, whereas Portfolio B has a standard deviation of 30 percent and a maximum loss of

20 percent. Thus, by either criterion of risk—standard deviation or maximum loss—Portfolio A is preferable to Portfolio B. If one flips a coin to decide between Portfolio A and Portfolio B, the whole process (flip a coin, then choose one portfolio or the other accordingly) has a lower standard deviation than just choosing Portfolio B, but the process has the *same maximum possible loss* as just choosing B. The most you can lose by either choice is 20 percent. Thus the maximum loss criterion violates the desideratum to prefer a chance of a better thing to the certainty of a worse thing. If one accepts the latter, then maximum loss is not even permitted into the contest between alternative risk measures.

This chapter generalizes this discussion. In roughly the following order, it:

- Defines certain concepts, including the expected utility maxim
- Describes the properties of expected utility maximization, including whether preferences determine utility numbers uniquely and what shape utility function encourages portfolio diversification
- Contrasts the HDM (human decision maker) with the RDM (rational decision maker), the latter being the topic of this book
- Discusses objections that have been raised to the expected utility rule and how these confuse the behavior observed in an HDM with that to be expected from an RDM

- Presents three decision-choice "axioms" that we believe it is reasonable to expect of an RDM
- Refers the reader to a proof [in Markowitz (1959)] that a decision maker who acts consistently with the aforementioned axioms must necessarily act according to the expected utility rule
- Ties up an important loose end

Subsequent chapters of this part of the book consider the merits of various risk-return criteria as approximations to the expected utility rule. As noted in the preface, subsequent parts are planned that will consider rational decision making over time with known odds, rational decision making when odds are not known, and certain implementation considerations, especially the division of labor among computers, data, algorithms, and judgment.

This chapter and the three that follow may all seem very academic, but the topics covered are, in fact, of central importance in practice. Few, if any, decisions are more important in the actual use of risk-return analysis than the choice of risk measure. A false statement on the subject—such as, "The use of variance as a risk measure assumes that return distributions are normally distributed"—can be stated in a fraction of a sentence and then left as self-evident, but an accurate, nuanced account of the topic—including a description of the boundaries where mean-variance (MV) approximations begin to break down—requires more space.

DEFINITIONS

In this section, we define the terminology used in our discussion of the maximum expected utility rule. Imagine an RDM who must choose between alternative probability distributions such as

Probability distribution P
$$= \begin{cases} \text{a 0.001 chance of winning \$1,000,} \\ \text{a 0.999 chance of winning nothing;} \end{cases}$$

Probability distribution Q
$$= \begin{cases} \text{a 0.01 chance of winning \$100,} \\ \text{a 0.99 chance of winning nothing} \end{cases}$$

After the RDM selects one such distribution, a wheel is spun and—eventually—the outcome is announced. The RDM can make no relevant decision between the choice of a probability distribution and the announcement of the outcome. This absence of possibly relevant intervening decisions characterizes this as a single-period choice situation. See Markowitz (1959), Chapter 11, the section entitled "Intermediate Decisions, Incomplete Outcomes" for an elaboration of this point.

We will speak of "outcomes," "probability distributions of outcomes," "preferences among probability distributions of outcomes," and "the expected utility maxim." By definition, *one and only one outcome* can occur. If it is possible, for example, for the individual to win both $1,000 and a car, then this combination is defined as a single outcome. If it is possible for the individual to neither win nor lose, this is defined as another outcome. We can imagine a situation whose outcomes, thus defined, are:

- Win a car
- Win $1,000
- Win both a car and $1,000
- Win nothing

These would be the four possible "outcomes" of the particular single-period choice situation.

It will be convenient to assume that there is only a finite number (n) of outcomes. This is not a serious practical limitation because n can equal the number of microseconds since the Big Bang. (We will cite literature that generalizes the results presented here to nonfinite probability distributions.) One may represent a probability distribution among the n possible outcomes by a vector:

$$P = (p_1, p_2, \ldots, p_i, \ldots, p_n)$$

where p_i is the probability that the ith outcome will be the one to occur. Since one and only one outcome will occur, the p_i sum to 1:

$$\sum_{i=1}^{n} p_i = 1 \qquad (1a)$$

and, of course, cannot be negative:

$$p_i \geq 0 \qquad i = 1, \ldots, n \qquad (1b)$$

One may think of two probability distributions,

$$P = (p_1, \ldots, p_n) \text{ and } Q = (q_1, \ldots, q_n)$$

as "lottery tickets" offering different probabilities of outcomes. One can imagine flipping a coin and then engaging in lottery P if heads appears or lottery Q if tails appears. If this is done, the probability of obtaining the ith outcome is

> (the probability of engaging in lottery P) times (the probability of obtaining outcome i if P is engaged in)

plus

> (the probability of engaging in lottery Q) times (the probability of obtaining outcome i if lottery Q is engaged in)

If the coin is fair, this equals

$$(1/2)p_i + (1/2)q_i$$

In general, if there is a probability (a) of engaging in P and a probability $(1 - a)$ of engaging in Q, then the probability of obtaining the ith outcome is

$$ap_i + (1 - a)q_i$$

The probability distribution of ultimate outcomes associated with a probability (a) of P and $(1 - a)$ of Q is therefore the probability distribution represented by the vector

$$[ap_1 + (1 - a)q_1, ap_2 + (1 - a)q_2, \ldots, ap_n + (1 - a)p_n]$$

In matrix notation, this is the vector denoted as $aP + (1 - a)Q$. Thus the latter may be interpreted either as a chance of P or Q or as a new vector of probabilities obtained from vectors P and Q by the rules of matrix algebra.

An implicit assumption of an analysis such as ours—which is frequently overlooked or underappreciated—is that a situation to be analyzed is set up so that the RDM's decisions do (and the HDM's decisions should) depend only on the probability distributions of outcomes *and not on how these probabilities are generated*. In particular, we assume that outcomes have been "suitably defined," that is, so that the decision maker is indifferent between (1) having an outcome generated by a single distribution with probabilities equal to $aP + (1 - a)Q$ and (2) the previously described two-stage process. If the decision maker enjoys the process itself, such as the watching of a horse race, then this must be accounted for in defining "outcomes." See Markowitz (1959 and 1997) for further elaboration of this point.

We consider an RDM who has preferences among probability distributions of the n outcomes. Specifically, if P and Q are any two such probability distributions, the

RDM either prefers P to Q, prefers Q to P, or considers both equally good. A set of preferences may or may not be in accordance with the expected utility maxim. If preferences are in accordance with the expected utility maxim, there are numbers

$$u_1, u_2, u_3, \ldots, u_n$$

such that the probability distribution

$$(p_1, \ldots, p_n)$$

is preferred to the probability distribution

$$(q_1, \ldots, q_n)$$

if and only if

$$\sum_{i=1}^{n} u_i p_i > \sum_{i=1}^{n} u_i q_i \qquad (2)$$

We call $u_1, u_2, \ldots$ the *utilities* assigned to each outcome. The average of these utilities, weighted by probabilities $p_1, p_2, \ldots$, is the distribution's expected utility. Thus the expected utility rule assumes that some *linear* function $\sum u_i p_i$ describes the RDM's preferences among probability distributions.

UNIQUENESS

If $u_1, u_2, \ldots, u_n$ are utility numbers that describe an RDM's preferences, and one computes new utility numbers $u'_1, \ldots, u'_n$ by multiplying the old utilities by a positive number and perhaps adding a constant:

$$u'_1 = a + bu_1,$$
$$u'_2 = a + bu_2,$$
$$\ldots,$$
$$u'_n = a + bu_n \quad b > 0 \quad (3)$$

then $u' = (u'_1, \ldots, u'_n)$ ranks probability distributions exactly as does $u = (u_1, \ldots, u_n)$. That is,

$$\sum u'_i p_i \geq \sum u'_i q_i \quad (4a)$$

if and only if

$$\sum u_i p_i \geq \sum u_i q_i \quad (4b)$$

Proof

$$EU' = \sum p_i u'_i$$
$$= \sum p_i (a + bu_i)$$
$$= a \sum p_i + b \sum p_i u_i$$
$$= a + bEU$$

But since $b > 0$, $E_P U' \geq E_Q U'$ if and only if $E_P U \geq E_Q U$.

If a decision maker had preferences among probability distributions of three outcomes with utilities $u_1 = 3$, $u_2 = 4$, and $u_3 = 8$, and it were desirable to describe these preferences in such a way that the utility attached to the first outcome is 0 and that attached to the third is 1, we may divide each utility by 5 and then subtract 3/5 to obtain equivalent utilities:

$$u'_1 = 0, u'_2 = 0.2, \text{ and } u'_3 = 1$$

The u' describe the same set of preferences as the u and have the specified outcomes as the "origin" and "unit" for their utility scale.

In general, any outcome can be assigned zero utility, and any preferred outcome can be assigned unit utility. Beyond that, the decision maker's preferences among probability distributions uniquely determine the utility number that must be assigned to each outcome. For example, suppose that an Outcome 1 is assigned zero utility and an Outcome 2 is assigned unit utility. What utility number or numbers may be assigned to an Outcome 3 that is preferred to Outcome 1 but not to Outcome 2? In a subsequent section, we will see that if the decision maker acts according to the expected utility maxim, there is a probability p such that the probability p of getting Outcome 1 and the probability $1 - p$ of getting Outcome 2 are exactly as good as getting Outcome 3 with certainty. Hence

$$\begin{aligned} u_3 &= pu_1 + (1-p)u_2 \\ &= p(0) + (1-p)(1) \\ &= 1-p \end{aligned}$$

This value of u_3 must be assigned to Outcome 3 to represent the RDM's preferences once $u_1 = 0$ and $u_2 = 1$ have been assigned. Other cases are dealt with in an endnote.[1]

CHARACTERISTICS OF EXPECTED UTILITY MAXIMIZATION

In the particular case in which random outcomes are the returns on a portfolio, the utility associated with various levels of return can be represented by a curve such as $\ell\ell'$ or ss' in Figure 1.1. (To be consistent with our assumption that there are only a finite number of possible outcomes, we can imagine that the curves in Figure 1.1 connect the utilities of various discrete levels of return, for example, from 100 percent loss to some huge gain, by increments of 0.0001 percent.)

A curve that is shaped like $\ell\ell'$ in Figure 1.1 is said to be *concave*; one that is shaped like ss' is called *convex*. The property that identifies a concave curve is that a straight line drawn between any two different points on the curve lies everywhere on or below the curve. If it actually lies below the curve everywhere, as it would in the case of $\ell\ell'$, we say that the curve is *strictly* concave. With a convex curve, a straight line drawn between two points of the curve lies everywhere on or above it. In the case of a *strictly* convex curve, the line lies above the curve everywhere.

Suppose that an individual who acts according to the strictly concave utility curve $\ell\ell'$ must choose between:

1. A 50-50 chance of a *gain* of (*a*) percent or a *loss* of (*a*) percent
2. The certainty of no change

The expected return in both cases is zero. Figure 1.1 is drawn so that the expected utility of option 2 is also zero. The utility attached to option 1 is

$$(1/2)U(a) + (1/2)U(-a)$$

This equals the utility level of the point (*b* on $\ell\ell'$, *c* on *ss'*) halfway between $[-a, U(-a)]$ and $[a, U(a)]$ of the respective curves. These lie on the straight lines connecting the points.

FIGURE 1.1 Convex and Concave Utility Curves.

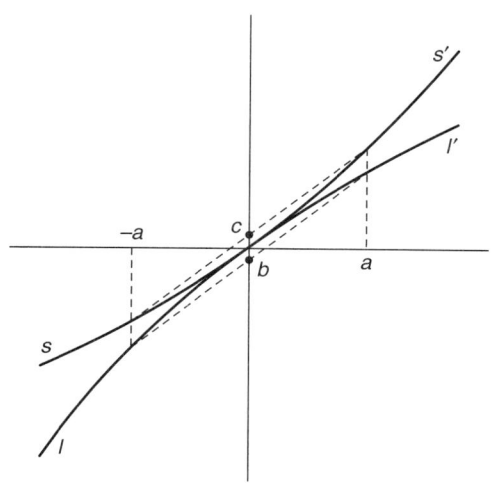

Because $\ell\ell'$ is strictly concave, the utility at b is less than zero: the certainty is preferred to the gamble. Thus an RDM with a concave utility function is risk-averse and will tend to prefer diversified portfolios. The implications of a convex utility curve such as ss' are the opposite. The expected utility at point c is greater than that of no bet. An RDM with a convex utility function would be a risk seeker and would not diversify his or her portfolio.

Unless otherwise specified, throughout this book we will assume that the decision maker under discussion has a strictly concave (and therefore risk-averse) utility function.

RDMs VERSUS HDMs

In a later section, we postulate, as "axioms," certain properties that we would expect of an RDM in making choices among risky alternatives. In some ways, an RDM is like an HDM; in other ways, the RDM and the HDM are quite different. Two ways in which the RDM and the HDM are alike are:

- The RDM cannot predict the outcome of a flip of a coin.
- Like an HDM, an RDM has objectives. Specifically, he or she would like a "good" probability distribution of the possible outcomes of any risky action that he or she takes.

A major difference between an RDM and an HDM is that the former computes instantly with no errors of logic or arithmetic, whereas most HDMs cannot—in their head, without a computer—compute the probabilities of relatively simple probabilistic outcomes, partly because they do not know the applicable formulas.

Another difference between an HDM and an RDM is that the HDM is subject to fuzziness of perception and the RDM is not. Specifically, we assume that *if* the RDM is indifferent between probability distributions P and Q, *and* indifferent between distributions Q and R, *then* the RDM will be indifferent between P and R. But such precision is not to be expected from an HDM. Humans do not show such precision, for example, in their perception of the intensity of light or the loudness of sound, so why should we expect it in their perception of their preferences? In particular, experimental evidence to the effect that human preferences are not transitive—that the human can prefer probability distribution P to Q and Q to R, but also R to P—are simply explained by assuming imprecision in the perception of the human's own preferences.

An HDM's imprecision in the perception of light or sound is approximately described by Weber's Law. This says that the increment in stimulus whose existence and direction can be identified correctly is proportional to the base level to which the increment is added. In other words, equal increments in the *logarithm* of the stimulus are perceived equally. This relationship has been observed to hold for a variety of stimuli, except at their extremes; for example, going from zero photons per second to one photon per second is not infinitely perceivable, even though $\log(0) = -\infty$.

Kontek (2011) uses Weber's Law to explain Kahneman and Tversky's (1979) data more simply than they did. Kontek applies Weber's Law to money amounts at stake; for example (in another context), a dime seems like a large amount when it is added to the price of a stick of gum but minuscule when it is added to the price of a mansion. (For another example, the first listed author of the present work—whom some might consider to be the very model of a rational decision maker—bought regular gas when gas was one or two dollars per gallon but currently often pays $4.60 for midgrade rather than $4.50 for regular "since there is hardly any difference." But he often thinks of Weber's Law when he does so.)[2]

While Kontek makes effective use of Weber's Law applied to payoffs, we will see that well-publicized differences between HDM behavior and the expected utility maxim can be explained by Weber's Law applied to the odds of gambles. This proposed application of Weber's Law has two caveats:

1. The first caveat is the usual one, that the law fails in extreme cases.

2. The perception of probability p as $\log(p)$ should apply to "small probabilities," that is, less than 0.5—perhaps well under 0.5.

Concerning the first caveat, since $\log(0) = -\infty$, for example, Weber's Law applied literally implies that the HDM can discriminate between $p = 0.0$ of winning a prize versus $p = \varepsilon > 0$ for any positive ε, no matter how small. As with the transition from zero to one photon per second, Weber's Law should not be pushed to this limit. But hundreds of thousands (perhaps millions) of HDMs *can* tell the difference between $p = 0$ and $p = 10^{-9}$ because they stand in line to buy state lottery tickets (say, for a dollar each) when the grand prize is in the hundreds of millions of dollars and the HDMs know that the state makes money on its lottery. Since many buy more than one ticket, they can discriminate between $(n-1)\varepsilon$ and $n\varepsilon$ for small n and $\varepsilon = 10^{-9}$. On the other hand, if someone already had a 50-50 chance of winning hundreds of millions of dollars, the thought furthest from their minds would be how to increase the odds from 0.500000000 to 0.500000001.

Concerning the second caveat, we assume that an HDM has some sense that if event E has probability p of occurrence, then the nonoccurrence of E should have, at least roughly, probability $1 - p$. It follows that if Weber's Law applies to p near zero, it cannot apply to p near 1.0. The example in the following text applies Weber's Law to probabilities p and q well below 0.5.

ALLAIS'S PARADOX

Objections have been raised to the expected utility maxim, including, in particular, those for which Maurice Allais won a Nobel Prize. Allais's objections involve cases in which human subjects, after careful deliberation, choose alternatives that are inconsistent with the expected utility maxim. The situations are fairly simple, the human choice quite definite, and the contradiction between the choice and the maxim inescapable. Thus one must conclude either that the expected utility maxim is not the proper criterion for rational behavior or that the HDM has a propensity toward irrationality, even in his or her most reflective moments.

Markowitz (1959), Chapter 10, presents three examples in which it is possible for an individual to prefer an alternative that is inconsistent with the expected utility maxim. In each case, the "wrong" alternative has a plausible appearance and is chosen by many test subjects. Two of Markowitz's (1959) examples are due to Allais (1953); the third, reproduced here, is based on the same principle but has a somewhat simpler structure. The conclusion that Allais drew from such examples is that since reasonable people choosing among simple alternatives contradict the expected utility maxim, this rule must not be essential to rational decision making. Markowitz (1959) draws a different conclusion. Here we repeat Markowitz's (1959) argument, augmented by the use of Weber's Law.

In the following example, an individual is given his or her choice of three lottery tickets. Lottery A has one chance in a thousand of winning $1,000, Lottery B has one chance in a hundred of winning $100, whereas Lottery C has one chance in two thousand of winning $1,000 and, in addition, one chance in two hundred of winning $100. Thus, the alternatives are:

Alternative	Chances (out of 2,000)	Outcome
A	2	$1,000
	1,998	0
B	20	$100
	1,980	0
C	1	$1,000
	10	100
	1,989	0

Subjects asked to choose among these often express a preference for C. Such a preference is inconsistent with the expected utility rule because

$$EU_C = \frac{1}{2,000} U(\$1,000) + \frac{1}{200} U(\$100) + \frac{1,989}{2,000} U(\$0)$$

$$= \frac{1}{2}\left[\frac{1}{1,000} U(\$1,000) + \frac{999}{1,000} U(0)\right]$$

$$+ \frac{1}{2}\left[\frac{1}{100} U(\$100) + \frac{99}{100} U(0)\right]$$

$$= \frac{1}{2} U_A + \frac{1}{2} U_B$$

Therefore, EU_C cannot be larger than both EU_A and EU_B.[3]

Which is wrong, the expected utility maxim or the individual who chooses C?

Those who respond with a preference for C may be further interrogated as to whether they prefer A to B or vice versa.

The argument is essentially the same whichever is chosen. For concreteness, assume that A is preferred to B. We may further inquire as to whether the person would rather have A with certainty or a 50-50 chance of obtaining A or B. The unanimous response of those who prefer A to B is that they would prefer to have A outright rather than a chance of A or B. The formula for computing the probabilities of final outcomes when a coin is flipped between two lotteries here yields

$$P_{\$1,000} = \frac{1}{2} \frac{2}{2,000} = \frac{1}{2,000}$$

$$P_{\$100} = \frac{1}{2} \frac{20}{1,000} = \frac{10}{1,000}$$

$$P_{00} = 1 - P_{\$1,000} - P_{\$100}$$

$$= \frac{1,989}{2,000}$$

Thus the probability distribution of outcomes from flipping the coin to choose A or B is exactly the same as the probabilities offered in C. It follows that *if in this situation, it is the probabilities of outcomes that determine choice—and not how these probabilities are generated—the respondent's choices are self-contradictory:*

> C is preferred to A.
> A is preferred to a 50-50 chance of A or B.
> But a 50-50 chance of A or B is exactly the same thing as C.
> Thus C is preferred to C—a contradiction.

For some situations—such as cheering on one's horse or playing cards with friends—the process itself adds to the player's utility. For the applications in this book, which concern an investor allocating serious money or a fiduciary advising such an allocation, the fun of the game should be a negligible consideration as compared to probabilities of returns.

WEBER'S LAW AND THE ALLAIS PARADOX

Weber's Law—applied to probabilities—explains the HDM's choices among Allais-type alternatives. Suppose, for example, that a decision maker can choose any probabilities p_0, p_1, p_2 that he or she wants for specified dollar outcomes

$$D_0 < D_1 < D_2$$

subject to the constraints that these are probabilities, that is,

$$p_0 + p_1 + p_2 = 1 \qquad (5a)$$
$$p_0 \geq 0 \quad p_1 \geq 0 \quad p_2 \geq 0 \qquad (5b)$$

and that they have a given expected value

$$p_0 D_0 + p_1 D_1 + p_2 D_2 = k \qquad (5c)$$

For example, if $D_0 < 0$ were the price of a lottery ticket with possible prizes D_1 and D_2, then $k = 0$ would define a "fair" lottery, while $k < 0$ would afford the lottery organizer a profit.

We may arbitrarily let the utilities of D_0 and D_2 be $u_0 = 0$ and $u_2 = 1$; then the utility of D_1 is $u_1 \in (0,1)$. For a typical lottery, $|D_0|$ is quite small as compared to D_1 and D_2. With $k \leq 0$, this implies that feasible p_1 and p_2 are small, with $p_1 + p_2$ well under 0.5, and therefore with p_0 well over 0.5.

An EU maximizer would choose p_0, p_1, p_2 so as to maximize

$$\begin{aligned} EU &= u_0 p_0 + u_1 p_1 + u_2 p_2 \\ &= u_1 p_1 + p_2 \end{aligned} \quad (5d)$$

subject to Constraints (5a) and (5b). Such an EU maximizer would never prefer probability allocation with $p_i > 0$ for $i = 0, 1, 2$. [This is a special case of a similar result with any number of prizes, proved in Markowitz (2010).] Since we know that for a typical lottery, $p_0 > 0$, it follows that, for such a lottery, an expected utility maximizing solution always exists with either $p_1 = 0$ or $p_2 = 0$. Thus, as in other Allais-type examples, a preference for $p_i > 0$ for $i = 1, 2, 3$ contradicts the expected utility maxim.

If Weber's Law applies to the perception of p_1 and p_2, then Objective Function (5d) becomes

$$V = u_1 \log(p_1) + \log(p_2) \quad (5e)$$

Note that this need not apply to p_0, since $u_0 = 0$.

The values of p_0, p_1, and p_2 that maximize V subject to Constraints (5a) and (5b) have $p_0 > 0, p_1 > 0, p_2 > 0$.

Proof

Using Equation (5a) to eliminate p_0 from Equation (5c), we obtain

$$p_1(D_1 - D_0) + p_2(D_2 - D_0) = (k - D_0) \tag{5f}$$

which we may write as

$$a_1 p_1 + a_2 p_2 = c \tag{5g}$$

where $a_1 > 0$, $a_2 > 0$, and $c > 0$ for the typical lottery. Setting to zero the partial derivatives of the following Lagrangrian:

$$L = V - \lambda(a_1 p_1 + a_2 p_2)$$

we find that

$$\frac{u_1}{p_1} = \lambda a_1 \tag{5h}$$

$$\frac{1}{p_2} = \lambda a_2 \tag{5i}$$

Therefore

$$p_1 = h u_1 / a_1 \tag{5j}$$

$$p_2 = h / a_2 \tag{5k}$$

where $h = 1/\lambda$. If Equations (5h) and (5i) have a solution, necessarily $\lambda \neq 0$. Substituting Equations (5j) and (5k) into Constraint (5g), we find that

$$h(1 + u_1) = c$$
$$h = c/(1 + u_1)$$
$$> 0$$

That this provides a maximum (rather than, for example, a minimum) follows from the fact that Equation (5g) can be used to express p_2 as a linear function of p_1, with $p_1 > 0$ at $p_2 = 0$ and $p_2 > 0$ at $p_1 = 0$. Thus Objective Function (5e) can be written as a function of p_1 that goes to $-\infty$ as $p_1 \to 0$ in one direction and as $p_2 \to 0$ in the other.

Thus Inequalities (5b) are satisfied by an internal maximum, illustrating that an HDM subject to Weber's Law in the perception of small probabilities may choose alternatives that are inconsistent with EU maximization when offered an Allais-type gamble.

THE AXIOMS

Euclid based geometry in particular, and much of the known mathematics at the time in general, on an "axiomatic" approach. He laid down certain axioms and postulates and deduced their consequences in his 13-volume tour de force. Von Neumann and Morgenstern (1944) introduced the axiomatic method into the area of immediate interest to us, namely, choice among alternative probability distributions. The von Neumann and Morgenstern axioms imply that one should act so as to maximize expected utility. Markowitz (1959), Chapter 10, presents two simpler sets of axioms, which are, in turn, variations of a set presented by Marschak (1950). Rather than distinguish axioms from postulates as Euclid did, the von Neumann and Morgenstern, Marschak, and Markowitz systems lay down axioms only and then deduce the consequences of these using accepted principles of mathematics and logic. This is because Euclid's *Elements* formalized much of then-known mathematics, including its rules of inference, whereas von Neumann and Morgenstern and others derive the consequences of their axioms using well-known mathematical procedures that, in turn, have their own (various alternative, much-debated) systems of axioms.

The two Markowitz (1959) axiom systems consist of the same Axioms I and II, plus either Axiom III or Axiom III'. These will be described in the following three sections. Proofs that these axiom systems imply the expected utility rule may be found in Markowitz (1959), Chapter 10 and Appendix C, together with proofs that certain "weakenings" of these systems would not imply the expected utility maxim.

AXIOM I

The first axiom asserts that an RDM can, in fact, order probability distributions and that this is a consistent ("transitive") ordering. Specifically:

> *Axiom I, Part A: If P and Q are any two probability distributions, then either P is preferred to Q, or Q is preferred to P, or both are considered equally good.*

Axiom I, Part B: If P is considered at least to be as good as Q and Q is considered at least as good as R, then P is considered to be at least as good as R.

Part A of Axiom I implicitly assumes that the situation has been analyzed so that preferences are based on probability distributions and not on the way those distributions are generated. It explicitly assumes that an RDM is not subject to indecision: either *P* is preferred to *Q*, or *Q* is preferred to *P*, or else the choice between them is a matter of indifference.

Part B may be put this way: we should be rather disappointed with an RDM portfolio advisor if he or she told us that Portfolio 1 is better than Portfolio 2, Portfolio 2 is better than Portfolio 3, and at the same time—with no change of information or circumstances—Portfolio 3 is better than Portfolio 1. In particular, Part B rules out fuzziness in the perception of preferences because it implies that if *P* is exactly as desirable as *Q* and *Q* is exactly as desirable as *R*, then *P* will be exactly as desirable as *R*. As noted previously, this is a major difference between an HDM and our idealized RDM.

AXIOM II

The second axiom concerns situations like the flipping of a coin between two lotteries, but is a bit more subtle. Specifically:

Axiom II: If Probability Distribution P is preferred to Probability Distribution Q, and if R is any probability distribution whatsoever, then a probability (a) of

obtaining P and a probability $(1 - a)$ of obtaining R is
preferred to a probability (a) of obtaining Q and a probability $(1 - a)$ of obtaining R—provided (a) is not zero.

Axiom II requires a word of explanation. Consider a situation in which there is a probability $(1 - a)$ of receiving Probability Distribution R and a probability (a) of having a choice of either Distribution P or Distribution Q. Axiom II is implied by our basic assumption—that the situation has been analyzed so that choice depends on probabilities and not on how these probabilities are generated—since always choosing P provides an overall distribution of $aP + (1 - a)R$, whereas always choosing Q provides an overall distribution of $aQ + (1 - a)R$.

In Axiom II, R may be any probability distribution. This implies two corollaries: first, if $R = P$, the axiom says that the certainty of P is better than a chance of Q, and second, if $R = Q$, the axiom says that a chance of P is better than the certainty of Q, as we presumed in an earlier example.

> A man walks into a restaurant and asks the waiter for coffee without cream. The waiter replies, "I'm sorry, sir, but we ran out of cream. Would you like your coffee without milk?"

Assuming that a request for coffee without cream is a way of expressing a preference for black coffee, P, over either coffee with milk, Q, or coffee with cream, R, the waiter in this tale thinks that the preference between P and Q may depend on the presence or absence of R. If this is absurd, then the logically equivalent objections to Axiom II are equally absurd. This does not imply that Allais was absurd to raise such objections. On the contrary, the Allais-style paradoxes have forced us to examine our assumptions about the RDM as compared to the actions of the HDM.

AXIOMS III AND III′

The two alternative third axioms of Markowitz (1959) assert, in effect, that the RDM's preferences are a continuous function of probabilities. One way to describe this is to say that preferences can be ordered by some function

$$f(p_1, \ldots, p_n)$$

where f is continuous. Another way of describing this (usually taken by axiomatic treatments of expected utility) assumes one or more properties of the RDM's preferences which, in turn, imply the existence of such a continuous ordering function.

It is possible to construct preference patterns that cannot be described by a continuous ordering function. For example, suppose that an individual prefers to have a candy bar to not having one; and prefers not to have a candy bar to being struck dead instantly. Suppose, further, that he or she must choose between

> A. Eating the candy bar with probability a and being struck dead with probability $(1 - a)$
> B. Being certain that neither of these happens

If the individual chooses B for all values of *a* less than 1, his or her preferences cannot be described by a continuous ordering function. But people do cross busy streets to buy a snack. When we say *any* probability less than 1.0, we include probabilities such as

0.9999999999999999999999999999999999995

Axioms III and III' rule out absolute safety-first behavior, like not crossing the street for a snack if there is any chance of being run down by a car or a truck.

> *Axiom III. If P is preferred to Q and Q is preferred to R, then there is a number (a) such that $aP + (1 - a)R$ is exactly as good as Q.*

> *Axiom III'. If Probability Distribution P is preferred to Probability Distribution Q and Probability Distribution Q is preferred to Probability Distribution R, then there are numbers $p < 1$ and $q > 0$ such that*
>
> (a) $pP + (1 - p)R$ *is preferred to Q.*
> (b) *Q is preferred to* $qP + (1 - q)R$.

Axiom III' formalizes the argument against discontinuities presented in the candy bar example. Axioms I, II and either III and III' are necessary and sufficient conditions for the applicability of the EU rule. Necessity is easy to show:

If an RDM acts according to the expected utility rule, his or her actions satisfy these axioms.

Proof

According to Inequality (2), the expected utility rule specifies that preferences among Probability Distributions P, Q, R, and so on are in accordance with some *linear* ranking function. Choice according to any ranking function $f(p_1, p_2, \ldots, p_n)$ satisfies Axiom I, any continuous function is consistent with Axiom III or III′, and the linearity of Inequality (2) ensures that Axiom II is satisfied.

Thus the three axioms constitute "necessary conditions" for the expected utility rule to hold. Markowitz (1959) shows the converse: that either set of three axioms is sufficient as well. The proofs there assume a finite number of possible outcomes. Extensions of the axiom systems to cover infinite numbers of possible outcomes are presented in Fishburn (1982), along with references to the developers of these systems. Unfortunately, Fishburn (1982) contains one egregious error. He ascribes his initial axiom system (for finite outcome populations) to Jensen (1967), when in fact it consists of our Axioms I, II, and III′, first presented in Markowitz (1959).

As already noted, an HDM's perceptions of his or her preferences are imprecise. This vagueness of perception would be a problem if our proposed use of the expected utility maxim were to explicitly formalize the investor's utility function and then choose portfolios that maximized its expected value. But our use of the expected utility maxim is quite different. Later chapters illustrate that for a wide range of concave utility functions, if an investor chooses an appropriate (for him or her) portfolio from a mean-variance efficient frontier, he or she will have achieved almost maximum expected utility—*without even knowing what his or her utility function is*! Not only is the loss in EU optimality not great in itself, but, we argue, it is insignificant when compared with the errors that must be expected from the forward-looking estimates of the parameters needed for a mean-variance analysis or the (usually more demanding) estimates that would be needed for a full expected utility analysis, and perhaps even as compared with the errors of perception discussed earlier.

BOUNDED VERSUS UNBOUNDED UTILITY OF RETURNS

We have completed the principal objective of this chapter, namely, to explain why we use the expected utility maxim as the touchstone for judging better and worse criteria for selecting portfolios. We now turn to the cleaning up of an important "loose end." Specifically, we will examine an apparent contradiction between what we have said previously and what we will later do.

The two axiom systems just presented hold if and only if preferences can be ordered by utility numbers $u_1, \ldots, u_n$, as in Inequality (2). The u_i are finite, of course. In fact (for $n \geq 3$), if one of the u_i equaled either ∞ or $-\infty$, it is an easy exercise to show that neither Axiom III nor III' can hold. But some of Chapter 2 and most or all of Chapters 3 and 4 are concerned with mean-variance approximations to the logarithmic utility function that, in the event of a 100 percent loss, has

$$U = \log(1.0 - 1.0) = -\infty$$

Furthermore, while cases with an infinite number of outcomes are beyond the scope of this book, we note that Menger (1967) has shown that if a utility function is unbounded either above or below, then a probability distribution can always be defined with either plus or minus infinity expected utility. Therefore, if there is an infinite number of possible outcomes, our axiom systems imply the existence of numbers $\underline{U}$ and $\overline{U}$ such that

$$\underline{U} \leq u_i \leq \overline{U} \quad \text{for all } i$$

But $\log(1 + R)$ is unbounded both above and below. So which is correct: bounded utility or the logarithmic utility function, and in either case, how do we reconcile Axiom III or III' with the contents of Chapters 3 and 4 of the present volume?

At this point, we reaffirm our acceptance of Axioms I, II, and III or III', hence utility that is bounded above and below. For example, suppose that one had a utility function that ascribed $U = -\infty$ to a 100 percent portfolio loss. This implies (assuming that the utility of a 99.99 percent loss is finite) that one would prefer to be certain of a 99.99 percent loss rather than have the slightest chance of being completely wiped out. We assume that the reader has no such preference. If we try to fix the problem by also ascribing a minus-infinity utility to a 99.99 percent loss, the problem is repeated in comparison with a 99.98 percent loss, and so on. This illustrates why we consider it plausible to insist that U be bounded below.

On the other hand, if an RDM had a utility function that was unbounded above, then no matter how much wealth one offered the RDM—for example, $\$10^9$, $\$10^{12}$, $\$10^{16}$, or more—there would be a greater wealth such that the RDM would trade certainty of the lesser amount (for example, $\$10^{12}$) for a small chance of the greater amount. Again, we assume that the reader has no such preference.

We use the logarithmic utility function in testing the efficacy of mean-variance approximations for three reasons:

1. Antiquity: the logarithmic utility function was the one that Daniel Bernoulli (1954) proposed in 1738 when he discovered problems with the expected income maxim.
2. In Chapter 4, we compare the performance of a mean-variance approximation to the expected log with that of approximations using alternative measures of risk. Some of these alternative measures are supposed to be superior to mean variance in the case of large deviations. An unbounded utility function seems appropriate in evaluating the efficacy of risk measures in the face of large deviations.
3. The expected log of a probability distribution (or the average log of a series) is known once its geometric mean is known, and vice versa. The geometric means

for the return series in two interesting databases are readily available, which lead to the writing of Chapter 3. After that, Chapter 4 (which required additional data) just *had* to be written.

We reconcile the axioms, which we accept, with the use of logarithmic utility throughout Chapters 3 and 4 by thinking of log utility itself as being an approximation to some true (usually unknown) utility function. All the probability distributions with which we will deal have their worst returns little, if any, greater than a 90 percent loss. It is sufficient, therefore, for the log utility function to be a good enough approximation (to some true, bounded utility function) over the range from a 90 percent loss to some very large gain. The results reported in Chapter 4 speak to the question of the efficacy of different measures of risk in approximating such a utility function over such a range.

POSTSCRIPT

It is frequently said that mean-variance analysis should not be used if distributions are not normal. The fact that Markowitz (1959) bases its support for mean-variance analysis on mean-variance approximations to expected utility is rarely cited. For example, Quiggin (1993), p. 8, says, "The EU approach initially faced strong competition from mean-variance analysis, exemplified by the work of Markowitz (1959) on portfolio analysis, but the logical foundations of this approach were far more dubious than those of expected utility theory." An examination of the Table of Contents of Markowitz (1959) would have revealed a chapter entitled, "Expected Utility." A cursory examination of this chapter would have shown that the premises of utility analysis and the premises that Markowitz (1959) proposed in support of mean-variance analysis are *identical.*

Quiggin is not alone in this mistaken notion about the fundamental assumptions of portfolio theory. These are widely held despite repeated attempts by Markowitz to spread the truth on this subject [as in Levy and Markowitz (1979), Kroll et al. (1984), Markowitz (1991a), Markowitz (1991b); Markowitz et al. (1994), Markowitz and Usmen (1996a, 1996b), Markowitz (1997), Markowitz and Usmen (2003), Markowitz and van Dijk (2003), and Markowitz (2010)].

We hope that the present volume will help spread the word as to the fundamental assumptions of Markowitz (1959) and, more important, the conditions under which mean-variance analysis will well serve actual investors.

2

MEAN-VARIANCE APPROXIMATIONS TO EXPECTED UTILITY

INTRODUCTION

In the preceding chapter, we explained why we accept the expected utility rule as the standard for rational choice among probability distributions. We also explained that in the case of probability distributions of portfolio returns, concave-shaped utility functions lead to risk-avoiding choices: given the choice between a particular return R with certainty versus a random outcome with R as its expected value, the decision maker who maximizes the expected value of a strictly concave utility function will prefer the certain to the random outcome. In this chapter and the next, we explore whether some function of mean and variance can provide a good approximation to the expected values of various concave utility functions. In Chapter 4, we consider whether functions of mean and risk measures other than variance can do a better job of approximating the expected value of a particular utility function.

A number of authors have asserted that a mean-variance (MV) efficient portfolio will give precisely optimum expected utility (EU) if and only if return distributions are normal or U is quadratic.[1] An implied corollary is that a well-selected point from the mean-variance efficient set can be trusted to yield almost maximum expected utility only under such severe restrictions. Since statisticians frequently reject the hypothesis that return distributions are normal, and since every concave quadratic eventually reaches a maximum and heads in the wrong direction, some writers conclude that mean-variance analysis should be rejected as the method for portfolio selection, no matter how economical it is as compared with alternative formal methods of analysis.

On the other hand, Markowitz (1959) asserts that if a utility function $U(R)$ can be approximated closely enough by a quadratic for a sufficiently wide range of returns, then EU will be approximately equal to some function $f(E,V)$ of expected return E and variance of return V. In particular, it suggests two methods for approximating a given utility function by a quadratic:

$$Q_Z(R) = U(0) + U'(0)R + 0.5U''(0)R^2 \qquad (1)$$
$$Q_E(R) = U(E) + U'(E)(R - E) + 0.5U''(E)(R - E)^2 \qquad (2)$$

where a prime denotes differentiation. For example, for the natural logarithm utility function $U = \log(1 + R)$, approximations (1) and (2) are, respectively,

$$q_Z(R) = R - \frac{1}{2}R^2 \qquad (3)$$

$$q_E(R) = \log(1 + E) + (R - E)/(1 + E)$$
$$- (R - E)^2/[2(1 + E)^2] \qquad (4)$$

Recalling that variance V is defined as $E(R - E)^2$, from which it follows that $V = ER^2 - E^2$, we see that the expected value of each of these equations is a function of mean and variance, namely,

$$f_Z(E, V) = E - (E^2 + V)/2 \qquad (5)$$
$$f_E(E, V) = \log(1 + E) - V/[2(1 + E)^2] \qquad (6)$$

As shown in Table 2.1, which is Table 2 on page 121 of Markowitz (1959), for returns between a 30 percent loss and a 40 percent gain *on the portfolio as a whole*, there is little difference between $\log(1 + R)$ and q_Z. For example, at $R = -0.30$ (a 30 percent loss), $\log(1 + R) = -0.36$, whereas the quadratic is -0.35. At $R = 0.40$ (a 40 percent gain), $\log(1 + R) = 0.34$, whereas the quadratic is 0.32. Between these two values, that is, for $R = -0.20, -0.10, \ldots, +0.30$, the approximation equals the log utility function to the two places shown. Even at a 40 percent loss or a 50 percent gain, the difference is noticeable but not great: -0.51 versus -0.48 in the one case; 0.41 versus 0.38 in the other. As the range of possible returns increases further, however, the approximation deteriorates at an increasing rate. In particular, $\log(1 + R)$ goes toward minus infinity as R approaches -1.0, a 100 percent loss, whereas q_Z goes to -1.5. Conversely, as R increases, q_Z reaches a maximum at $R = 1$ and then heads downward.

TABLE 2.1 Comparison of $\text{Log}(1 + R)$ with $R - 1/2\,R^2$

R	Log(1 + R)	R − 0.5 R²
−0.50	−0.69	−0.63
−0.40	−0.51	−0.48
−0.30	−0.36	−0.35
−0.20	−0.22	−0.22
−0.10	−0.11	−0.11
0.00	0.00	0.00
0.10	0.10	0.10
0.20	0.18	0.18
0.30	0.26	0.26
0.40	0.34	0.32
0.50	0.41	0.38

Markowitz (1959) concludes that among return distributions that are mostly within the range of a 30 percent loss to a 40 percent gain on the portfolio as a whole and do not fall outside this range too far, too often, the $E[\log(1 + R)]$ maximizer will almost maximize expected utility by an appropriate choice from the mean-variance efficient frontier. Subsequently, various authors have tested the ability of functions of mean and variance to approximate expected utility for various utility functions and historical or postulated portfolio return distributions. By and large, their conclusions have been favorable.

The present chapter surveys this research, with attention to negative as well as positive conclusions concerning the existence of functions $f(E,V)$ that approximate various EU.

WHY NOT JUST MAXIMIZE EXPECTED UTILITY?

If one believes that action should be in accordance with the maximize EU rule, why seek to *approximately* maximize it via a mean-variance analysis? Why not just maximize expected utility? In addressing this question, we distinguish three types of expected utility maximization:

- Explicit
- MV-approximate
- Implicit

We refer to it as *explicit* EU maximization when a utility function is given and analytical or numerical methods are used to find the portfolio that maximizes the expected value of this function. In contrast, we refer to it as *MV-approximate* EU maximization when a utility function is given and a mean-variance approximation to its expected utility is maximized. An example would be to approximately maximize $E \log(1 + R)$ by generating an MV efficient frontier and choosing from it the portfolio that maximizes f_Z or f_E in Equation (5) or Equation (6).

As reviewed in this chapter, Levy and Markowitz (1979) find that mean-variance approximations are usually quite accurate. From this they conclude, for some hypothetical investor Mr. X, that "If Mr. X can carefully pick the MV efficient portfolio which is best for him, then Mr. X, who still does not know his current utility function, has nevertheless selected a portfolio with maximum or almost maximum expected utility." We refer here to such a process as *implicit* expected utility maximization.

Typically, it is much more convenient and economical to determine a set of mean-variance efficient portfolios than it is to find the portfolio that maximizes expected utility. Historically, one source of inconvenience and added expense for the latter was computational. One typically had to wait longer (perhaps hours longer) and pay a higher computer bill to find an expected utility maximizing portfolio than to trace out a mean-variance frontier. This computational problem is now trivial thanks to faster, cheaper computers. It still takes many times as long to compute the expected value of most concave functions as it does to trace out a mean-variance efficient frontier.[2] But neither calculation takes long enough to be a practical limitation.

There are, however, other expenses and inconveniences that remain involved in explicitly maximizing expected utility as compared with using an MV or implicit approximation to it. The first of these concerns parameter estimation. The only inputs required for a mean-variance analysis are the means, variances, and covariances of the securities or asset classes of the analysis. (A factor model can serve in place of individual variances and covariances.) This is because the formulas relating the expected return and variance of a portfolio to the expected values, variances, and covariances of the returns of securities do not depend on the form of the probability distribution. Letting E_p be the expected return of the portfolio; X_i, the fraction of the portfolio invested in the ith security; and E_i, the expected return of the ith security or asset class, the relationship

$$E_p = \sum_{i=1}^{n} X_i E_i \qquad (7)$$

is true whether or not returns are normally distributed, or even symmetrical, and whether or not the return distributions have "fat tails," as long as the E_i exist and are finite. Similarly, letting V_p be the variance of the portfolio and σ_{ij} be the covariance between security returns r_i and r_j, the formula for portfolio variance

$$V_p = \sum_{i=1}^{n}\sum_{j=1}^{n} X_i X_j \sigma_{ij} \qquad (8)$$

is true whether or not the return distributions are symmetrical or have fat tails, as long as the V_i are finite.

The case is different when one explicitly maximizes expected utility. Then one must determine what type of joint probability distribution generates return combinations $(r_1, r_2, \ldots, r_n)$ and must estimate the parameters for such a joint distribution. Accomplishing this can require a substantial research project, as Chapter 5 illustrates.

A second difficulty with using explicit expected utility maximization, as opposed to implicit EU maximization, is that someone must determine the investor's utility function. As von Neumann and Morgenstern (1944) explain, theoretically this should be done by having the investor answer a series of questions as to what probabilities p_a of returns R_a versus $(1 - p_a)$ of R_c the investor considers just as desirable as return R_b with certainty for various returns R. This would be challenging enough for an institutional investor, such as an endowment or pension fund with a single large portfolio, but seems hardly possible in any thorough way on behalf of the many clients of a financial advisor. This step is not necessary when implicit EU maximization is used.

Finally, another advantage of using implicit EU maximization is that no one has to explain the expected utility concept to the individual investor, to the supervisory board of an institutional investor, or to the typical financial advisor. Instead, portfolio choice can be couched in the familiar terms of risk versus return.

UTILITY OF RETURN VERSUS UTILITY OF WEALTH

Equations (3) and (4) assume that an investor seeks to maximize the expected value of $\log(1 + R)$, where R is the return on the portfolio during the forthcoming period.[3] Instead, suppose that one assumed that the investor seeks to maximize the expected value of some function of end-of-period wealth W_{t+1}. The latter is connected to return and beginning-of-period wealth W_t by the formula

$$W_{t+1} = (1 + R)W_t \tag{9}$$

Mean-Variance Approximations to Expected Utility · 45

In the case of a log utility function, the portfolio that maximizes $E\log(W_{t+1})$ also maximizes $E\log(1 + R)$ because Equation (9) implies that

$$\log(W_{t+1}) = \log(1 + R) + \log(W_t) \tag{10}$$

When the portfolio to be held from time t to $t + 1$ is chosen, W_t is already given, and therefore, $\log(W_t)$ is a constant as far as this choice is concerned. As we saw in Chapter 1, if two utility functions U and V are related linearly,

$$V = a + bU \qquad b > 0 \tag{11}$$

the probability distribution that maximizes EU also maximizes expected variance (EV). Thus Equation (10) implies that the same portfolio is chosen among those available whether one maximizes $\log(1 + R)$ or $\log(W_{t+1})$.

Next, consider the power utility function

$$U = X^a \qquad \text{for } a > 0 \tag{12a}$$

or

$$U = -X^a \qquad \text{for } a < 0 \tag{12b}$$

For example,

$$U = X^{1/2} \tag{12c}$$

or

$$U = -X^{-\frac{1}{2}} \quad (12d)$$

As in the case of the log utility function, a power utility function implies the same choices among probability distributions whether one lets X be W_{t+1} or $(1 + R)$ in Equations (12a) and (12b) because for example,

$$(W_{t+1})^a = (1+R)^a W_t^a \quad (13)$$

Since W_t is already determined when the probability distribution of R (or W_{t+1}) is chosen, the condition in Equation (11) applies.

Equations (10) and (13) also imply that—for the power or log utility functions—the choice of portfolio does not depend on the level of start-of-period wealth W_t. This is not true for all utility functions. In particular, it is not true of the exponential utility function

$$\begin{aligned} U &= -\exp(aW_{t+1}) \\ &= -\exp[aW_t(1+R)] \end{aligned} \quad (14)$$

because this is of the form

$$U = -\exp[-b(1+R)] \quad (15)$$

where b depends on W_t. A subsequent section will illustrate the dependence on b of choice among probability distributions by an investor with an exponential utility function.

If Equation (14) were the investor's utility of wealth function, and if it remained constant through time, the investor's single-period utility of return function in Equation (15) would change from one period to the next. Mean-variance approximation has no difficulty with this. The basic assumption is *not* that $U(R)$ stays the same with time but that at any one time EU can be adequately approximated by some function of E and V. In particular, $U(R)$ could change with the investor's age and circumstances as well as his or her wealth.

LOISTL'S ERRONEOUS ANALYSIS

In a paper entitled "The Erroneous Approximation of Expected Utility by Means of a Taylor's Series Expansion: Analytic and Computation Results," Loistl (1976) concludes that "the mean-variance approximation is not a good approximation of the expected value of utility at all" (p. 909). The reason Loistl reaches such a negative conclusion is as follows: note that in Table 2.1, a 10 percent return is represented as $R = 0.10$, not as $R = 10.0$. In particular, in Equation (9), if starting wealth is $W_t = \$1,000,000$ and the portfolio returns 10 percent, then ending wealth is

$$W_{t+1} = 1,000,000 \cdot (1 + 0.10)$$
$$= 1,100,000$$

not

$$W_{t+1} = 1,000,000 \cdot (1 + 10)$$
$$= 11,000,000$$

Loistl assumes that utility U is a function of a random variable y, "where y is the investor's wealth" (p. 905). He gives an example in which "return in percent" is listed as $-20, -10, \ldots,$ 30, 40. He then compares $U(y)$ with different Taylor series approximations, including the quadratic, fit with $X_0 = \bar{y}$, for $y = -20, y = -10, \ldots, y = 40$, confining the comparisons with $y > 0$ for the logarithmic utility function. In other words, Loistl represents a 30 percent gain by $R = 30$ rather than by $R = 0.3$. Loistl's conclusion—that the quadratic approximation fits poorly for these values of y—is consistent with the Markowitz (1959) observation that a quadratic fits well for returns in the interval -0.3 to 0.4. Since a 30 percent gain must be represented by $R = 0.3$ rather than $R = 30$ in the calculation of end-of-period wealth W_{t+1}, as in Equation (9), or its end-of-period expected utility, as in Equation (10), Loistl's negative conclusion about mean-variance approximation is due to an erroneous analysis rather than an erroneous approximation.

LEVY AND MARKOWITZ (1979)

The Levy-Markowitz study had two principal objectives:

1. To see how good mean-variance approximations are for various utility functions and portfolio return distributions
2. To test an alternative way of estimating expected utility from a distribution's mean and variance

The Levy-Markowitz "alternative way" was to fit a quadratic approximation to U at three values of R:

$$(E - k\sigma), (E), (E + k\sigma)$$

They tried their approach for

$$k = 0.01, 0.1, 0.6, 1.0, \text{ and } 2.0$$

Of these, $k = 0.01$ did best in almost every case. This is essentially the same as the approximation in Equation (2). We will therefore relate their results for $k = 0.01$ and subsequently treat these as if they were results for the Equation (2) approximation.

Table 2.2 shows the Levy-Markowitz results for four data sets. The first column of the table lists various utility functions. The next shows results based on the annual returns for 149 mutual funds for the years 1958 through 1967—namely, all the mutual funds whose returns were reported for the full period in the then latest edition of Wiesenberger (1941). Levy and Markowitz considered these 149 return series as 149 real-world return distributions. Specifically, the table's second column presents correlations between average utility

$$\text{EU} = \sum_{t=1}^{T} U(r_t)/T \tag{16}$$

and the mean-variance approximation $f(E,V)$ based on the quadratic fit through the three points with $k = 0.01$.

TABLE 2.2 Correlations between EU and $f_{0.01}(E, V)$ for Four Historical Distributions 1958–1967

Utility Function	Annual Returns of 149 Mutual Funds	Annual Returns on 97 Stocks	Monthly Returns on 97 Stocks	Random Portfolios of Five or Six Stocks
$\mathrm{Log}(1 + R)$	0.997	0.880	0.995	0.998
$(1 + R)^a$				
$a = 0.1$	0.998	0.895	0.996	0.998
$a = 0.3$	0.999	0.932	0.998	0.999
$a = 0.5$	0.999	0.968	0.999	0.999
$a = 0.7$	0.999	0.991	0.999	0.999
$a = 0.9$	0.999	0.999	0.999	0.999
$-e^{-b(1 + R)}$				
$b = 0.1$	0.999	0.999	0.999	0.999
$b = 0.5$	0.999	0.961	0.999	0.999
$b = 1.0$	0.997	0.850	0.997	0.998
$b = 3.0$	0.949	0.850	0.976	0.958
$b = 5.0$	0.855	0.863	0.961	0.919
$b = 10.0$	0.447	0.659	0.899	0.768

The utility functions used were the logarithm, and the power and exponential functions for the values of a and b are shown in the table. For the logarithmic utility function and for all the power utility functions considered, the correlation (over the 149 return distributions) between average utility and the mean-variance approximation to average utility was at least 0.997. Since this is more precision than one should expect from forward-looking estimates of means, variances, and covariances for a mean-variance analysis—or from estimates of joint distributions for an explicit expected utility maximization analysis—Levy and Markowitz conclude that, for these utility functions and return distributions, for all practical purposes, EU and its mean-variance approximation are indistinguishable. On the other hand, the MV approximation was much less successful for exponential utility,

$$U = -\exp[-b(1 + R)]$$

for $b = 5$ and, especially, for $b = 10$. We will consider such utility functions at length later in this chapter.

The other columns of Table 2.2 show the correlation between EU and $f_{0.01}$ for three more sets of historical distributions reported by Levy and Markowitz. The second data set reported in the table shows such correlations for annual returns on 97 randomly chosen U.S. common stocks during the years 1948 to 1967. It is understood, of course, that mean-variance analysis is to be applied to the portfolio as a whole rather than to individual investments. Annual returns on individual stocks were used, however, as examples of return distributions with greater variability than that found in the portfolios reported in the prior column. As expected, the correlations were poorer for individual stocks than for mutual fund portfolios. For $U = \log(1 + R)$, for example, the correlation was 0.880 for the annual returns on stocks

52 • Risk-Return Analysis

as compared with 0.997 for the annual returns on the mutual funds.

Since monthly returns tend to be less variable than annual returns, we would expect the correlations to be higher for the former than for the latter—and, indeed, they are. The correlations between EU and $f_{0.01}$ for monthly returns on the same 97 stocks are shown in the fourth column of Table 2.2. For the logarithmic utility function, for example, the correlation is 0.995 for the monthly returns on individual stocks as compared with 0.880 for annual returns on the stocks and 0.997 for annual returns on the mutual funds. On the whole, the correlations for the *monthly* returns on individual stocks are comparable with those for the *annual* returns on mutual funds.

As noted previously, annual returns on individual stocks—that is, on completely undiversified portfolios—have perceptibly smaller correlations between EU and $f_{0.01}$ than do the annual returns on the well-diversified portfolios of mutual funds. The final column of Table 2.2 presents correlations for "slightly diversified" portfolios consisting of a few stocks. Specifically, it shows the correlations $\rho_{0.01}$ between EU and $f_{0.01}$ on the annual returns for 19 portfolios of five or six stocks, each randomly drawn (without replacement) from the 97 U.S. stocks. We see that for the logarithmic utility function, $\rho_{0.01} = 0.998$ for the random portfolios of five and six stocks, up from 0.880 for individual stocks. Generally, the $\rho_{0.01}$ for the annual returns on the portfolios of five and six stocks were comparable with those for the annual returns on the mutual funds. These results were among the most surprising of the entire analysis. They indicate that, as far as the applicability of mean-variance analysis is concerned, at least for joint distributions like the historical returns on stocks for the period analyzed, a little diversification goes a long way.

HIGHLY RISK-AVERSE INVESTORS

The Levy-Markowitz results for exponential utility with $b = 10$ differ markedly from those of the other utility functions reported in Table 2.2. In this section, we explore the reason for this.

For $E = 0.1$ and $\sigma = 0.15$, Table 2.3 compares the exponential utility function with the quadratic approximation Q_E in Equation (2). The utility function is rescaled as follows:

$$U = -1{,}000 e^{-10(1+R)}$$

With this scaling, the difference between $U(0.5)$ and $U(-0.3)$ is of the same order of magnitude as that for $\log(1 + R)$ in Table 2.1, namely, $0.41 - (-0.36) = 0.77$ in the latter case versus about 0.91 in the former. Table 2.3 is presented to four places rather than two, as in Table 2.1, because $U(R)$ rounds to 0.00 to two places for $R \geq 0.3$ for the exponential.

The first column of Table 2.3 lists R; the second, $U(R)$; the third, the quadratic approximation Q_E; and the fourth column presents the difference between utility U and the quadratic Q_E,

TABLE 2.3 Comparison of Exponential Utility with a Quadratic Approximation for $U = -1{,}000e^{-10(1+R)}$, $E = 0.10$, and $\sigma = 0.15$

R	U(R)	$Q_E(R)$	$U - Q_E$
−0.30	−0.9119	−0.2171	−0.6948
−0.20	−0.3355	−0.1420	−0.1935
−0.10	−0.1234	−0.0835	−0.0399
0.00	−0.0454	−0.0418	−0.0036
0.10	−0.0167	−0.0167	0.0000
0.20	−0.0061	−0.0084	0.0022
0.30	−0.0023	−0.0167	0.0144
0.40	−0.0008	−0.0418	0.0409
0.50	−0.0003	−0.0835	0.0832

namely, $d_E(R) = U(R) - Q_E(R)$. The table sheds light on why a quadratic approximation does much better for $\log(1 + R)$ than for $-\exp[-10(1 + R)]$. In Table 2.1, the maximum difference between $\log(1 + R)$ and $Q_Z(R)$ is 0.02. In Table 2.3—with U scaled for comparability with Table 2.1—the absolute value of the difference $|d_E|$ is 0.69 at $R = -0.3$. Thus the immediate reason that $f(E,V)$ is not a good approximation to EU in this case is that its Q_E is not a good approximation to $U(R)$. And the reason for that is that this $U(R)$ turns too quickly in the neighborhood of $R = E$. Between $R = -0.30$ and $R = 0.10$, utility increases by about 0.90 from $U(-0.3) = -0.912$ to $U(0.1) = -0.017$. But since $U \leq 0.0$ everywhere, it becomes comparatively flat as R increases further. Specifically, it rises less than 0.02 between $R = 0.10$ and "$R = \infty$." Essentially, $U(R)$ has a knee at $R = E$.

Levy and Markowitz observe that an investor who had $-e^{-10(1+R)}$ as his or her utility function would have some strange preferences among probabilities of return. Since $U(R) < 0$ for all R, it follows that

$$0.5U(0.0) + 0.5U(R) < -0.0227 < U(0.1) \quad \text{for all } R$$

Therefore, the investor would prefer

A 10 percent return with certainty

to

A 50-50 chance of zero return (no gain, no loss)
versus a gain of 10^9 percent or more

Put another way, such an investor would prefer 10 percent with certainty to a 50-50 chance of either breaking even or getting a "blank check." Markowitz, Reid, and Tew (1994) find that real investors do not have such a low "value of a blank check" (VBC). In their survey of brokerage customers, the median value of VBC was 401 percent as a fraction of the investor's portfolio or 143 percent as a fraction of the investor's total wealth, well above the less than 10 percent VBC of the exponential with $b = 10$.

HIGHLY RISK-AVERSE INVESTORS AND A RISK-FREE ASSET

Simaan (1993) explores the efficacy of MV-approximate maximization for investors with the exponential utility function when a risk-free asset is available versus when such a risk-free asset is not available. He finds that, for investors with exponential utility functions with large values of b, MV-approximate EU maximization is highly efficacious when a risk-free asset is available and much less so when it is not.

In deriving these results, Simaan assumes that security returns follow a factor model,

$$1 + r_i = a_i + b_i F + u_i \qquad i = 1, \ldots, n \qquad (17)$$

where the u_i are normally distributed, not necessarily independently, and F is a (skewed) random variable with a Pearson Type III distribution. (The various types of Pearson distributions are discussed in Chapter 5 of this volume.) Simaan also assumes that the only constraint on portfolio choice is

$$\sum_i X_i = 1$$

Given these assumptions, Simaan is able to solve for the optimum portfolio.

Simaan illustrates these results based on monthly returns for 10 randomly selected securities. The measure of efficacy used by Simaan is what he calls the "optimization premium," namely, the return θ that would have to be added to the

TABLE 2.4 Simaan's Optimization Premiums

b	No Risk-Free Asset	With Risk-Free Asset
2	0.00023	0.00050
4	0.00073	0.00025
6	0.00144	0.00017
8	0.00229	0.00012
10	0.00323	0.00010
15	0.00581	0.00007
20	0.00859	0.00005
25	0.01147	0.00004
50	0.02646	0.00002
100	0.05719	0.00001

MV-approximate maximum portfolio to make it as desirable for the investor as the explicit optimum.

Table 2.4 presents the Simaan results. The first column shows the coefficient b in the exponential utility function; the second column shows the optimization premium when a risk-free asset is *not* available; the third column shows the optimization premium when a risk-free asset *is* available. For example, for $b = 10$, if there is no risk-free asset, one would have to add 0.00323, that is, roughly 3/10 of 1 percent, of the value of the portfolio *each month* to make it just as good as the explicitly maximized portfolio, whereas if a risk-free asset is available, only 0.0001, that is, one basis point per month, need be added. Clearly, if one wishes to serve highly risk-averse investors, one should make a risk-free asset available.

PORTFOLIOS OF CALL OPTIONS

It is often said that mean-variance analysis is not valid if it is applied to portfolios that contain securities with asymmetrical distributions, or whose returns vary in a nonlinear manner as a function of some security or index. Hlawitschka (1994) examines the efficacy of mean-variance and higher-order approximations to expected utility for portfolios of calls and concludes that the aforementioned view is wrong.

For his individual stock return series, Hlawitschka uses the monthly returns for 10 years on 11 equally weighted portfolios, each containing 20 randomly chosen stocks. His call return series assumes that each call was 5 percent out of the money when purchased and was priced according to the Black-Scholes model. Hlawitschka's call portfolios include a 10 percent position in T-bills to avoid being wiped out in the event that all calls expire worthless.

Hlawitschka's principal results are shown in our Tables 2.5 and 2.6. The first column of Table 2.5 lists various utility functions; the second column shows the Spearman *rank* correlation coefficients between the actual average utilities and the quadratic Taylor-series approximations; the third column shows the Spearman coefficients between EU and a third-order approximation. The final two columns of the table show such information for the portfolios of call options.

TABLE 2.5 Spearman Rank Coefficients between $E[U(W)]$ and Taylor-Series Approximations

Utility Function	Portfolios of Common Stocks		Portfolios of Calls	
	Second-Order Approximation	Third-Order Approximation	Second-Order Approximation	Third-Order Approximation
$U(W) = \log W$	1.0000	1.0000	0.9727	−0.8636
$U(W) = W^{0.1}$	1.0000	0.9909	0.9818	−0.8182
$U(W) = W^{0.5}$	1.0000	1.0000	0.9545	−0.2091
$U(W) = W^{0.9}$	1.0000	1.0000	0.9545	0.6909
$U(W) = -e^{-0.1W}$	1.0000	1.0000	0.9818	1.0000
$U(W) = -e^{-W}$	1.0000	1.0000	0.9273	−0.3545
$U(W) = -e^{-5W}$	0.9909	0.9909	0.8364	−0.8545
Average	0.9987	0.9974	0.9441	−0.2013

TABLE 2.6 Correlations between $E[U(W)]$ and Taylor-Series Approximations

Utility Function	Second-Order Approximation	Third-Order Approximation	Fourth-Order Approximation	Fifth-Order Approximation	Sixth-Order Approximation
Individual Common Stocks					
$U(W) = \log(W)$	0.9986	0.9991	0.9990	0.9995	0.9997
$U(W) = W^{0.5}$	0.9997	0.9999	0.9999	0.9999	0.9999
$U(W) = -e^{-W}$	0.9989	0.9999	0.9999	1.0000	1.0000
Individual Call Options					
$U(W) = \log(W)$	0.8764	−0.7527	0.7304	−0.7054	0.7469
$U(W) = W^{0.5}$	0.7469	−0.5296	0.5628	−0.5503	0.5466
$U(W) = -e^{-W}$	0.7823	−0.6234	0.6193	−0.5858	0.5738

The results in Table 2.5 concerning portfolios of stocks seem even better than those in Levy and Markowitz. In particular, in six of seven cases, the correlation is perfect. In the seventh case, the exponential utility with $b = 5$, the rank correlation exceeds 0.99. One reason for these high correlations is that Hlawitschka uses monthly returns. As our Table 2.2 shows, MV approximations are quite close to EU for monthly return series, even for individual securities. Another reason for the high correlations is that these are rank correlations; therefore, as long as EU and its MV approximation produce the same ordering of the 11 portfolios, the rank-order correlation is 1.0. A rationale for using the Spearman rank-order correlation coefficient, rather than the usual Pearson correlation coefficient as Levy and Markowitz did, is that if an approximation orders probability distributions correctly, it will guide choice correctly.

The final two columns of Table 2.5 show that, as expected, the quadratic approximation to EU does less well for portfolios of call options than for portfolios of stocks. Nevertheless, the approximation is not bad. In the first five cases, the coefficient exceeds 0.95; in the sixth, it exceeds 0.92; and in the troublesome exponential case with $b = 5$, the coefficient rounds to 0.84.

The real surprise in the table is the unreliability of the third-order Taylor approximation. In particular, in five of the seven cases, the correlation coefficient is negative! This is further explored by Hlawitschka in his Table 5, reproduced here as our Table 2.6, and his Table 6 (not reproduced here, but we will quote Hlawitschka's conclusions from it). In our Table 2.6, the first column lists utility functions, and the following five columns show rank correlations for second-, third-, fourth-, fifth-, and sixth-order Taylor-series approximations. The first three rows show such coefficients for returns on individual stocks (rather than portfolios); the second triplet of rows shows them for individual call options. For monthly returns on individual stocks, the quadratic approximation is quite good, with rank-order correlation coefficients exceeding 0.998 in all three cases and with the higher-order approximations doing even better.

The last three rows of Table 2.6 show that the quadratic approximation does less well for monthly returns on portfolios consisting of 90 percent individual call options and 10 percent T-bills than it did for individual stocks. Specifically, the three rank-order correlation coefficients round to 0.88, 0.75, and 0.78. But the third- and fifth-order approximations were negatively correlated with EU, whereas the fourth- and sixth-order approximations had positive correlations but ones inferior to the quadratic.

Hlawitschka's concluding paragraph is as follows:

Recall that, although a series may ultimately converge, little can be said about any of its partial series; convergence of a series does not imply that the terms immediately decrease in size or that any particular term is sufficiently small to be ignored. Indeed, it is possible, as demonstrated here, that a series may appear to diverge before ultimately converging in the limit. The quality of moment approximations to expected utility that are based upon the first few terms of a Taylor series, therefore, cannot be determined by the convergence properties of the infinite series. This is an empirical issue, and empirically, two-moment approximations to the utility functions studied here perform well for the task of portfolio selection. *(Emphasis added.)*

EDERINGTON'S QUADRATIC AND GAUSSIAN APPROXIMATIONS TO EXPECTED UTILITY

Ederington's (1995) principal results are summarized in our Table 2.7, extracted from Ederington's Table 5. Ederington refers to the series represented in the table as "semi-ex ante simulated returns." He argues that historical return series such as those used by Levy and Markowitz are "ex post" samples drawn from some unknown population. Other possible samples from this same population might have randomly drawn more extreme returns than the one actual historical series and therefore would have been less conducive to quadratic approximation. Ederington's solution is as follows:

> [Q]*uarterly return data for 130 mutual funds over the ten-year period 1970–1979 were obtained from Wiesenberger Investment Companies Services' Management Results publication. For each fund* i, *we*

TABLE 2.7 Correlations of Ederington's Semi-Ex Ante Simulated Returns MV Approximations

Utility Function	Normality Assumption	Quadratic Assumption	Actual Four Moments
$\text{Log}(b + R)$			
$b = 1.0$	0.9969	0.9993	0.9995
$b = 2.0$	0.9997	0.9999	0.9999
$b = 0.9$	0.9958	0.9984	0.9992
$(1 + R)^b$			
$b = 0.1$	0.9977	0.9995	0.9997
$b = 0.5$	0.9996	0.9999	0.9999
$b = 0.9$	0.9999	0.9999	0.9999
$(2 + R)^b$			
$b = 0.1$	0.9998	0.9999	0.9999
$b = 0.5$	0.9999	0.9999	0.9999
$-(1 + R)^{-b}$			
$b = 0.5$	0.9908	0.9961	0.9980
$b = 1.0$	0.9837	0.9864	0.9947
$b = 2.0$	0.9723	0.9289	0.9796
$b = 3.0$	0.9303	0.7893	0.9286
$b = 4.0$	0.7701	0.5325	0.7699
$b = 5.0$	0.4721	0.2324	0.4819
$-e^{-b(1+R)}$			
$b = 0.1$	0.9999	0.9999	0.9999
$b = 0.5$	0.9999	0.9999	0.9999

(continued)

TABLE 2.7 (Continued)

Utility Function	Normality Assumption	Quadratic Assumption	Actual Four Moments
$b = 1.0$	0.9986	0.9995	0.9999
$b = 2.0$	0.9844	0.9979	0.9987
$b = 3.0$	0.9639	0.9907	0.9906
$b = 4.0$	0.9539	0.9664	0.9748
$b = 5.0$	0.9516	0.9201	0.9568
$b = 6.0$	0.9469	0.8526	0.9369

simulate 10,000 yearly returns by choosing four quarterly returns (r_1, r_2, r_3, r_4) at random from the set of 40 and calculating the yearly return R_i as:

$$(1 + R_i) = (1 + r_{i1})(1 + r_{i2})(1 + r_{i3})(1 + r_{i4})$$

This bootstrap like procedure may be termed a semi-ex ante (as opposed to purely ex post) method of comparing EU and MV. If market participants hold subjective probability distributions analogous to the distributions from which the quarterly returns are drawn and view these returns as serially independent, the set of simulated years should approximate their subjective distributions of yearly returns.

Ederington's synthetic series *do* include cases that are more challenging to MV approximation than those of Levy and Markowitz's historical series. But, while details vary, our Table 2.7 shows that utility functions that did well in the Levy and Markowitz experiments also did well in Ederington's experiment.

The first column of Table 2.7 lists utility functions, including a number that are not included in the Levy-Markowitz study. The second and third columns show correlations with two different MV approximations. The second of these is based on the second-order Taylor-series approximation in our Equation (2); the first is a function of mean and variance based on what Ederington refers to as a "near normality assumption." Specifically, Ederington's near-normality assumption uses the fourth-order Taylor approximation, but rather than using the third and fourth moments

$$M_3 = E(R-E)^3$$
$$M_4 = E(R-E)^4$$

of the actual return distribution, he assumes

$$M_3 = 0$$
$$M_4 = 3V$$

as is the case for a normal (Gaussian) distribution. This provides a "fourth-order approximation" that is a function of E and V only.

Kroll, Levy, and Markowitz (1984) had shown that many of the return series they used were probably not drawn from normal distributions. Ederington's position on such results was essentially this: true return distributions are not exactly normal, but neither are utility functions exactly quadratic. Therefore, leave it up to the data to tell us which method of approximation works best.

The final column of Table 2.7 shows correlations of EU with the expected value f, a fourth-order Taylor approximation using the distribution's actual M_3 and M_4. The table reports the correlations for Ederington's 22 utility functions to four places, as he did, for the reader's detailed examination. Our own "takeaway" from Ederington's table is as follows: in 14 of the 22 cases, the MV approximation based on the quadratic in our Equation (2) had a correlation with EU of over 0.99. In 12 of these 14 cases, the approximation based on near normality also had a correlation exceeding 0.99, including 4 cases in which all three approximations had a correlation of 0.9999. In the other 2 cases (in which the quadratic approximation had a correlation exceeding 0.99), the near-normality approximation had correlations rounding to 0.98 and 0.96. Thus, in the 14 cases in which MV quadratic approximation did exceedingly well, the near-normality approximation did about as well, and there was little room for improvement by using the distribution's actual M_3 and M_4.

This leaves eight cases in which the MV quadratic approximation had a correlation with EU of less than 0.99. Ignoring the case in which both the quadratic and the near-normality approximations have correlations in excess of 0.98, we are left with seven "challenging" cases. An interesting pattern appears in each of these. While all three approximations deteriorate:

- The quadratic approximation does worse than the other two.
- The near-normality approximation does roughly as well as the fourth-degree approximation using the series' actual M_3 and M_4.

For example, for $-\exp[-6(1 + R)]$, the correlations (for the nearly normal, quadratic, and fourth-order approximations, respectively) are

$$0.95 \qquad 0.85 \qquad 0.94$$

whereas for $-(1 + R)^{-5}$, they are

$$0.47 \qquad 0.23 \qquad 0.48$$

Generally, as b increases, the near-normality approximation holds up better than the quadratic approximation and does roughly as well the fourth-degree approximation using the actual M_3 and M_4. Therefore, confining ourselves to Ederington's three approximations to expected utility, there is little advantage to considering moments higher than mean and variance. For utility functions with medium to high VBC, the quadratic approximation does so well that there is little room for a fourth-order approximation to do perceptibly better, whereas for utility functions with low VBC, the near-normality approximation does about as well as the fourth-order Taylor approximation using the distribution's own M_3 and M_4.

OTHER PIONEERS

Previous sections reviewed what we consider to be the most critical steps toward our present understanding of MV approximations of EU. These include the Levy-Markowitz observation that MV approximations of EU are quite good for many standard concave $U(R)$, except those with extremely high risk aversion, that is, that have implausibly low VBC; Simaan's observation that such investors will nevertheless be well served if the MV analysis includes a risk-free asset; Hlawitschka's observation that MV approximations work for portfolios of calls; and Ederington's observation that functions of mean and variance other than ones based on a quadratic approximation to $U(R)$ may work well for utility functions with implausibly low VBC, even without a risk-free asset. Along the way, we have skipped over important contributors because, for example, their contributions principally confirmed the results already obtained with other databases or points of view. This section attempts to fill in some of these omissions.

Young and Trent (1969) were the first, after Markowitz (1959), to explore the efficacy of various mean-variance (and higher-order) approximations to $E\log(1 + R)$ or, equivalently, to the geometric mean. Based on monthly historical return series, they concluded that the Markowitz (1959) quadratic approximation in our Equation (2) did as well as any of the other quadratic approximations they tried and that higher-order approximations added little.

Levy and Markowitz (1979), discussed in a previous section, assumed that if EU and $f(E,V)$ were highly correlated, then $f(E,V)$ would provide near maximum EU. Kroll, Levy, and Markowitz (1984) used the historical returns on 20 randomly selected stocks to explore how close maximum $f(E,V)$ is to explicitly maximized EU among portfolios on an MV-efficient frontier. They found that it does quite well.

How to measure the efficacy of approximation has been an ongoing topic in this literature. In particular, Dexter, Yu, and Ziemba (1980) use the percent difference in "certainty-equivalent" wealth as their measure of MV efficacy. The Dexter et al. conclusion was that "In all cases $\left[W_C^E \text{ and } W_C^M \right]$ were virtually identical"; that is, the maximum-certainty equivalent was little greater than the mean-variance approximation.

Hakansson (1971) explored the efficacy of mean-variance approximation to $E\log(1 + R)$ for portfolios made up of one risk-free asset and two hypothetical stocks whose returns—one with probabilities of 100 percent loss versus 50 percent gain, the other with probabilities of 15 percent gain versus 165 percent gain—are well beyond the range where the quadratic in Table 2.1 fits well. Not surprisingly, Hakansson finds that mean-variance approximations are not efficacious in this case. Generally, analyses based on historical portfolio returns reported that MV approximations did well. Those that used made-up return distributions (of which Loistl's is the most extreme) found distributions where MV approximations broke down.

Grauer (1986) considers the efficacy of MV approximation to the power or logarithmic utility function when the investor can borrow all he or she wants at the risk-free rate, as permitted in the Sharpe-Lintner Capital Asset Pricing Model [see Mossin (1966)]. Grauer reports unfavorable results unless constraints are added to the mean-variance optimization to avoid bankruptcy. The Simaan analysis, reported previously, also found poor results for the exponential utility function for b smaller than the $b \geq 2$ cases reported in Table 2.6. He observed that the portfolios in these cases involved, simultaneously, extremely large short and long positions. He concluded that the constraint set he used—without nonnegativity constraints to permit analytic solution—did not produce real-world-relevant results for these values of b.

Pulley (1983) found that:

investors maximizing expected logarithmic utility would hold virtually the same portfolios as investors maximizing certain mean-variance functions [based on] exact empirical distributions of security returns. Moreover, we find the goodness of the mean-variance approximations to be robust for different holding periods, different ratios of noninvested to invested wealth, and different subjective return distributions, including nonnormal distributions.

The next two chapters of this volume report that certain MV approximations to expected logarithmic utility are efficacious for return distributions that are much more spread out than those to which Markowitz (1959) thought MV analysis applicable on the basis of our Table 2.1.

CONCLUSION

It is now more than half a century since Markowitz (1959) first defended MV analysis as a practical way to approximately maximize EU. In light of repeated confirmation since then of the efficacy of MV approximations to EU, the persistence of the Great Confusion—that MV analysis is applicable in practice only when return distributions are Gaussian or utility functions quadratic—is as if geography textbooks of 1550 still described the Earth as flat.

3

MEAN-VARIANCE APPROXIMATIONS TO THE GEOMETRIC MEAN

INTRODUCTION

Summaries of return series typically report their "geometric mean" return as well as their arithmetic mean. In general, if $A_1, \ldots, A_n$ are n nonnegative numbers, their geometric mean is defined as the nth root of their product,

$$\text{GM} = \sqrt[n]{A_1 \cdot A_2 \cdots A_n} \qquad (1a)$$

This is to be distinguished from their arithmetic mean, or ordinary average,

$$\text{AM} = (A_1 + A_2 \cdots + A_n)/n \qquad (1b)$$

The so-called geometric mean return in financial summaries is not literally the geometric mean of the return series

$r_1, r_2, \ldots, r_T$. (It couldn't be, since returns are sometimes negative.) Rather the reported geometric mean of the series (g_s) satisfies

$$1 + g_s = \sqrt[T]{(1 + r_1)(1 + r_2)(1 + r_3)\cdots(1 + r_T)} \qquad (2)$$

Thus, when one says that a return series had a 10 percent geometric mean, it means that $(1 + 0.1) = 1.1$ was the geometric mean of its $(1 + \text{return})$ series.

Assuming no subsequent deposits or withdrawals after an initial deposit, W_0, a bank that paid g_s per period would provide the same final wealth, W_T, as a portfolio with returns of $r_1, r_2, \ldots, r_T$. This may be seen as follows: after T periods, the investor's wealth is

$$W_T = W_0(1 + r_1)(1 + r_2)\cdots(1 + r_T) \qquad (3)$$
$$= W_0 \prod_{t=1}^{T}(1 + r_t)$$

Equation (2) implies that

$$(1 + g_s)^T = \prod_{t=1}^{T}(1 + r_t) \qquad (4)$$

From this and Equation (3), it follows that

$$W_T = W_0(1 + g_s)^T \qquad (5)$$

Thus, as asserted, the return g_s compounded T times yields the same final wealth as did the given return series.

In particular, W_0 yields W_T by compounding the *geometric mean* of the series rather than compounding its *arithmetic mean* A_S. Because of Equation (5), g_S is sometimes referred to as the *growth rate* or *internal rate of return* of the series. While Equation (4) expresses g_S as a function of the entire return series, $r_1, \ldots, r_T$, Equation (5) shows that only W_T/W_0 is needed to compute g_S.

It can be shown that

$$A_S \geq g_S \tag{6a}$$

with

$$A_S > g_S \tag{6b}$$

as long as the standard deviation of the series is greater than zero. (See Hardy, Littlewood, and Pólya, 1999). Thus the average rate of return of the series, A_S, overstates the internal rate of return achieved by the series.

If a probability distribution of returns R consists of n equally likely values, $v_1, \ldots, v_n$, then the geometric mean g of the probability distribution may be defined, analogously to g_S in Equation (2), as

$$1 + g = \sqrt[n]{(1 + v_1)(1 + v_2)\cdots(1 + v_n)} \tag{7}$$

But how should g be defined if the distribution does not consist of equally likely values? Toward this end, take the logarithm (to any base) of both sides of Equation (2) to get

$$\log(1 + g_S) = \sum_{t=1}^{T} \log(1 + r_t)/T \qquad (8a)$$

Thus the log of $1 + g_S$ is the average of the logs of (1 + return). Analogously, we *define*

$$\log(1 + g) = E \log(1 + R) \qquad (8b)$$

Since this holds for logarithms to any base—such as the natural logarithm, $\log_e$, as well as the common logarithm, $\log_{10}$—the studies reported in the previous chapter concerning mean-variance (MV) approximations to $E \log(1 + R)$ $[= E \log_e(1 + R)]$ are also studies of the ability of a function of mean and variance to approximate g.

If a series $r_1, r_2, \ldots, r_T$ were independent draws of the random return R, the "law of large numbers" would ensure that

$$\text{Avg}[\log(1 + R)] \rightarrow E \log(1 + R) \qquad (9)$$

Therefore, $g_S \rightarrow g$ with probability equal to 1.0. (See Breiman, 1960.) Equations (5), (8b), and (9) may be summarized thus: "in the long run, one gets the geometric mean return, not the arithmetic mean return."

The present chapter includes historical comparisons between g and mean-variance approximations to it. Unlike those in Chapter 2, the arithmetic and geometric means reported in this chapter were not computed to test the efficacy of mean-variance approximation. Rather, they are the arithmetic and geometric means, and the standard deviations, of return series that are collected because of interest in the series themselves, and for which arithmetic and geometric means are routinely computed. Specifically, we consider the efficacy of mean-variance approximations to g for two data sets. One consists of the historical returns on asset classes widely used in asset allocation decisions. The second contains the real returns during the twentieth century of the equity markets of 16 countries, as reported by Dimson et al. (2002).

In addition to the methods of approximation used for utility functions in general, as reported in Chapter 2, this chapter also considers the efficacy of mean-variance approximations proposed specifically for g. As explained later, the inputs and outputs of a mean-variance analysis must necessarily be estimated *arithmetic* rather than *geometric* means. But the investor or investment advisor should be provided with an estimated geometric mean, since that is the likely "return in the long run." Thus, the approximations tested in the present chapter support practice in three ways. First, they are further tests of the efficacy of MV approximations to expected utility—in this case, to the expected value of the log utility function via Equation (8b). Second, they show (for distributions like those of the historical series reported here) whether the arithmetic mean and variance outputs of an MV analysis can be used to estimate the portfolio geometric mean with reasonable accuracy. Third, they consider which of six MV approximations proposed for g have worked best historically. In the next chapter, we compare the efficacy of the mean-variance approximation with comparable approximations based on often-proposed alternative measures of risk.

WHY INPUTS TO A MEAN-VARIANCE ANALYSIS MUST BE ARITHMETIC MEANS

The inputs to a mean-variance optimizer must be the (estimated forthcoming) expected (that is, *arithmetic* mean) returns rather than the (estimated forthcoming) *geometric* mean returns. This is because it is true that the expected (or arithmetic mean) value of a weighted sum of random variables is the weighted sum of their expected values, as in Equation (7) of Chapter 2, but it is *not* true that the geometric mean of a weighted sum is the weighted sum of their geometric means.

This nonlinearity of the geometric mean is illustrated by the example in the following table:

Probability	Return R	$10R$
½	0.09	0.90
½	−0.05	−0.50
E	0.020	0.200
g	0.018	−0.025

The first two columns of the table show the probabilities and possible outcomes of a return distribution R with a 50-50 chance of a 9 percent gain or a 5 percent loss. The third column shows 10 times R, that is, the possible outcomes of a bet that leverages the returns in Column 2 tenfold (at zero interest cost). The expected value of R is 0.02; its geometric mean is

$$g(R) = \sqrt{(1.09)(0.95)} - 1$$
$$= 0.018$$

Levered tenfold, $E(10R) = 10E(R)$, but

$$g(10R) = \sqrt{(1.90)(0.5)} - 1$$
$$= -0.025$$

With tenfold leverage, the *arithmetic* mean of $10R$ is 10 times that of R, but the *geometric* mean is negative!

This illustrates that g is not a linear function of portfolio holdings: in this case, $g(10R) \neq 10g(R)$. More generally, if $g_s^1, g_s^2, \ldots, g_s^n$ are estimates of the geometric means of several securities or asset classes, there is no way to infer the growth rate of a *portfolio* of these asset classes from this information only. In particular, the growth rate of the portfolio, $g(\sum_i X_i r_i)$, will exceed that of the weighted average of the g_s, weighted by portfolio holdings, $\sum X_i g(r_i)$. Fernholz and Shay (1982) call this difference the *excess growth* of the portfolio and show that this "excess growth" can be approximated by a function of the covariance matrix alone.

We now consider how well six different functions of arithmetic mean and variance would have approximated the geometric means of various historical return series.

SIX MEAN-VARIANCE APPROXIMATIONS TO g

Table 3.1 reports summary statistics for various U.S. asset classes [as reported in Ibbotson (2010)], plus developed non-U.S. markets (EAFE) and emerging markets (EM) obtained from Morningstar's *EnCorr*. Table 3.4, in a subsequent section, shows the same information for real returns from the stock markets of 16 countries during the 101 years from 1900 through 2000 as reported by Dimson, Marsh, and Staunton (2002). We use nominal returns in Table 3.1, since this is the way portfolio returns are usually reported. We use real returns in Table 3.4 because the period includes the German hyperinflation, in which nominal return reached 310 billion percent in 1923. In such a situation, the important question is not whether the portfolio will grow by billions of percent, but whether it will keep up with inflation.[1]

In both tables, the name of the return series is in the first column; its arithmetic mean, standard deviation, and geometric mean are reported in the next three columns; and the fifth through tenth columns report the result of six different mean-variance approximations to g. Columns 11 through 16 of the tables show the difference between the approximations in Columns 5 through 10, respectively, and the actual geometric mean shown in Column 4. Summary

TABLE 3.1 Geometric Mean Approximations to Various U.S., EAFE, and EM Return Indices

Series	Arith. Mean	Std. Dev.	Geom. Mean	Q0	QE	EDD	LMT	NLN	HL	Q0 Error	QE Error	EDD Error	LMT Error	NLN Error	HL Error
Large-cap stocks	11.8	20.5	9.8	9.4	9.9	9.8	9.7	10.0	9.9	−0.4	0.1	0.0	−0.1	0.2	0.1
Small-cap stocks	16.6	32.8	11.9	10.3	12.1	11.6	11.2	12.2	11.9	−1.6	0.2	−0.3	−0.7	0.3	0.0
Long-term corp. bonds	6.2	8.3	5.9	5.8	5.9	5.9	5.9	5.9	5.9	−0.1	0.0	0.0	0.0	0.0	0.0
Long-term gov. bonds	5.8	9.6	5.4	5.3	5.4	5.4	5.3	5.4	5.4	−0.1	0.0	0.0	−0.1	0.0	0.0
Intermed.-term gov. bonds	5.5	5.7	5.3	5.3	5.3	5.3	5.3	5.3	5.3	0.0	0.0	0.0	0.0	0.0	0.0
U.S. Treasury bills	3.7	3.1	3.7	3.6	3.7	3.7	3.7	3.7	3.7	−0.1	0.0	0.0	0.0	0.0	0.0
Inflation	3.1	4.2	3.0	3.0	3.0	3.0	3.0	3.0	3.0	0.0	0.0	0.0	0.0	0.0	0.0
EAFE	12.6	23.1	10.2	9.6	10.3	10.1	9.9	10.3	10.2	−0.6	0.1	−0.1	−0.3	0.1	0.0
EM	20.0	37.5	13.8	11.6	14.3	13.5	13.0	14.5	14.0	−2.2	0.5	−0.3	−0.8	0.7	0.2
									Avg.	−0.6	0.1	−0.1	−0.2	0.1	0.0
									Avg. abs.	0.6	0.1	0.1	0.2	0.2	0.1
									Max. abs.	2.2	0.5	0.3	0.8	0.7	0.2
									Number of times best	2	5	6	4	5	8

Source: Morningstar's *Stocks, Bonds, Bills, and Inflation* and Morningstar's *EnCorr*.

statistics at the bottom of Columns 11 through 16 show for each method:

- The average error of approximation
- The average absolute error of approximation
- The maximum absolute error
- The number of times the method had the smallest error or was tied for the smallest error

Shaded cells indicate that the method had the smallest error or was tied for the smallest error for the particular series.

The six approximations are labeled Q0, QE, EDD, LMT, NLN, and HL. The approximate values of g computed using these six methods will similarly be labeled as g_{Q0}, g_{QE}, and so on. The remainder of this section defines these six approximations.

Approximations Q0 and QE in Columns 5 and 6 of each table are obtained by exponentiating the two approximations to $E \log(1 + R)$ in Equations (5) and (6) of Chapter 2, proposed in Chapter 6 of Markowitz (1959), namely,

$$g_{Q0} = \exp\left[E - \tfrac{1}{2}(\sigma^2 + E^2)\right] - 1 \qquad (10a)$$

$$g_{QE} = \exp\left[\log(1 + E) - \tfrac{1}{2}\sigma^2/(1 + E)^2\right] - 1 \qquad (10b)$$

(In the present calculations, E, of course, represents the historical average rather than the expected value.)

The EDD approximation in Column 7 is

$$g_{EDD} = \exp\left[\log(1+E) - \tfrac{1}{2}\sigma^2/(1+E)^2 \\ -0.75\sigma^4/(1+E)^4\right] - 1 \quad (10c)$$

This is the exponentiated version of the fourth-degree approximation to $E \log(1+R)$ proposed by Ederington (1995). Recall from Chapter 2 that this assumes that

$$E(R - ER)^3 = 0$$
$$E(R - ER)^4 = 3V^2$$

as with a normal distribution. The approximation in Column 8 is

$$g_{LMT} = E - \frac{1}{2}\sigma^2 \quad (10d)$$

This simple formula—often used for "back of the envelope" calculations—follows from Equation (10a) if one assumes that E^2 and g^2 are negligible. In particular, it approximates $\log(1+g)$ by g. We refer to this as the LMT (for limit) approximation, since it is generally correct in the limit as the holding period interval, Δt, approaches zero.

The approximation in Column 9 shows what g would be if $\log(1+R)$ were normally distributed, namely,[2]

$$1 + g_{NLN} = (1+E)/\sqrt{1 + V/(1+E)^2} \quad (10e)$$

We refer to this as the NLN (near lognormal) approximation.

Column 10 in each table shows what g would be, as a function of E and V, for a distribution with two equally likely outcomes. Specifically,

$$(1 + g_{HL})^2 = (1 + E)^2 - V \qquad (10f)$$

since

$$(1 + g_{HL}) = \sqrt{(1 + E + \sigma)(1 + E - \sigma)}$$

Jean and Helms (1983) ascribe this (as a mean-variance approximation to g) to Henry Latané. We therefore label it the HL approximation.[3]

The inputs and outputs of the approximation formulas, Equations (10a) through (10f), are fractions (like 0.06) rather than percentages (like 6.0). However, they are reported as percentages in Tables 3.1 and 3.4 for convenience of interpretation.

OBSERVED APPROXIMATION ERRORS FOR ASSET CLASSES

The only approximation errors in Tables 3.1 and 3.4 that exceed a whole percentage point are the Q0 approximations to the small-cap series (error = -1.6 percent) and to the emerging market series (error = -2.2 percent) in Table 3.1. Also, Q0 is the only one of our six approximation formulas that is not exactly right for all values of E when $V = 0$. Q0 is of historical interest: it and QE were the first mean-variance approximations to expected utility proposed [in Markowitz (1959)] as justifications for mean-variance portfolio analysis. It may still be of expository value, since it is derived from

$$\log(1 + R) \cong R - \frac{1}{2}R^2 \tag{11a}$$

which is simpler than QE's

$$\log(1 + R) \cong \log(1 + E) + (R - E)/(1 + E) \\ - \frac{1}{2}(R - E)^2/(1 + E)^2 \tag{11b}$$

But, for the reasons cited earlier in this paragraph, Q0 should not be relied on in practice. Our further analysis of the efficacy of mean-variance approximations to the geometric mean will usually not include Q0.

Figure 3.1 plots approximation error versus standard deviation, as shown in Columns 3 and 12 through 16 of Table 3.1. (If Q0 errors had been reported in Figure 3.1, the figure would have to have been rescaled to accommodate Q0's maximum error.) The errors plotted in the figure differ from those shown in the table due to rounding.

The arithmetic means, standard deviations, and geometric means in the table are shown to one-place accuracy, as reported in the table's sources. This is a reasonable practice, since reporting such numbers to the hundredth of a percent suggests greater accuracy than is to be expected from a mean-variance analysis in practice. In Table 3.1, the approximation values and their errors are also reported to one place. But the Excel computation of these numbers was

FIGURE 3.1 Approximation Errors versus Standard Deviation, Various Asset Class Returns.

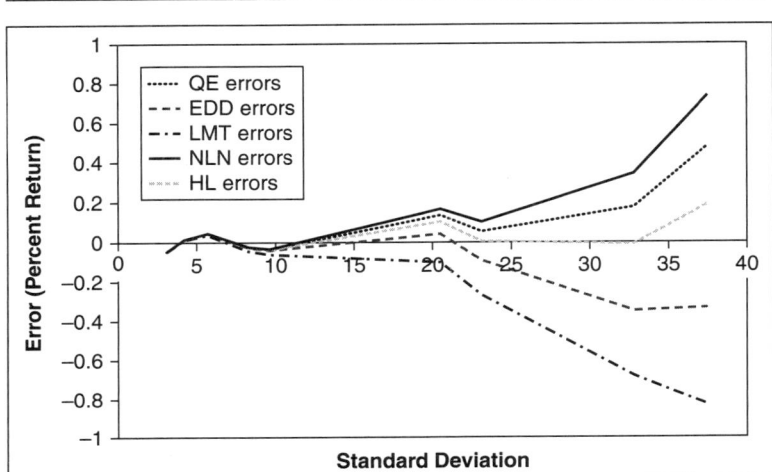

carried out to more places, and it is the errors thus computed that are plotted.

Table 3.2 shows these error values to three places, sorted by standard deviation. The table also contains summary numbers for each series (row) and each method (column). Specifically, Table 3.2 shows at the bottom of each column the average error (Avg.), the average absolute error (Avg. Abs.), and the maximum absolute error (Max. Abs.) for each method, and shows for each series (row) the average of the errors made by the different methods, the smallest (Min.) and largest (Max.) value of Error = estimate − actual, and the Range of errors, that is, Max − Min.

Figure 3.1 shows that the range of errors tends to increase with standard deviation. This is a mathematical

TABLE 3.2 Table 3.1 Errors to Three Places, Sorted by Standard Deviation

Standard Deviation	QE Errors	EDD Errors	LMT Errors	NLN Errors	HL Errors	Avg.	Min.	Max.	Range
3.1	−0.046	−0.046	−0.048	−0.046	−0.046	−0.047	−0.048	−0.046	0.002
4.2	0.014	0.014	0.012	0.015	0.014	0.014	0.012	0.015	0.003
5.7	0.046	0.045	0.038	0.046	0.046	0.044	0.038	0.046	0.009
8.3	−0.024	−0.027	−0.044	−0.023	−0.025	−0.029	−0.044	−0.023	0.022
9.6	−0.035	−0.040	−0.061	−0.033	−0.036	−0.041	−0.061	−0.033	0.028
20.5	0.136	0.043	−0.101	0.167	0.104	0.070	−0.101	0.167	0.268
23.1	0.055	−0.091	−0.268	0.103	0.005	−0.039	−0.268	0.103	0.371
32.8	0.177	−0.348	−0.679	0.344	−0.008	−0.103	−0.679	0.344	1.023
37.5	0.481	−0.333	−0.831	0.738	0.190	0.049	−0.831	0.738	1.569
Avg.	0.089	−0.087	−0.220	0.145	0.027	−0.009	−0.220	0.145	0.366
Avg. abs.	0.113	0.110	0.231	0.168	0.053	0.135	0.053	0.231	0.178
Max. abs.	0.481	0.348	0.831	0.738	0.190	0.518	0.190	0.831	0.641

Sums and differences may not check because of rounding.

relationship rather than an empirical one: If f and h are two mean-variance approximations to the geometric mean, and E_S, V_S, and g_S are the arithmetic mean, the variance, and the geometric mean of a series s, then the difference in the errors made by f and h is:

$$\Delta = [f(E_S, V_S) - g_S] - [h(E_S, V_S) - g_S]$$
$$= f(E_S, V_S) - h(E_S, V_S)$$

This is a function of the arithmetic mean as well as the variance of the series, but not of the observed g_S. The empirical content in Figure 3.1 is that—for the asset class series listed in Table 3.1—all five approximations do well for series with small standard deviations—with zero errors when rounded to one-tenth of 1 percent return—whereas for all series with higher standard deviations, the range of estimates brackets the observed g, with some methods overestimating and others underestimating the actual g.

For the series in Figure 3.1, the HL method performed best. Among the series with larger standard deviations and visibly higher ranges of estimates, it was always the median estimate (for reasons discussed in the next section). When observations are rounded to 0.1 of 1 percent, as in Table 3.1, the HL method is closest or tied for closest in eight out of nine cases. Its maximum absolute error of 0.2 of 1 percent is smaller than that of any other method.

Table 3.3 provides a tabulation of the absolute values of the errors of the five approximations. In most cases, the

TABLE 3.3 Frequencies of Table 3.1 Errors

Abs. Error	QE	EDD	LMT	NLN	HL
0.0	5	6	4	5	7
0.1	2	1	2	1	1
0.2	1			1	1
0.3		2	1	1	
0.4					
0.5	1				
0.6					
0.7			1	1	
0.8			1		

absolute error rounded to 0.3 of 1 percent or less; in four cases it rounded to 0.5 to 0.8 of 1 percent. We see in Table 3.3 that the absolute error of HL rounded to 0.0 in seven out of nine series, and (as noted earlier) in no case rounded to more than 0.2 of 1 percent. This is rather remarkable, since it is often assumed that return distributions are skewed to the right and are leptokurtic, whereas the HL approximation is derived from (and is exactly correct for) a distribution that is symmetric and has minimum kurtosis, that is, is as platykurtic as possible.

As noted earlier, for the series in Table 3.1 and Figure 3.1, the HL approximation did best. Arguably, EDD did second best. Its absolute error rounded to zero in six out of nine cases and never rounded to more than 0.3 of 1 percent. If EDD is awarded second place, then third place must go to QE. All of its absolute errors rounded to 0.2 of 1 percent or less, except one (emerging markets) that rounded to one-half of 1 percent.

All NLN errors either rounded to zero or were positive, indicating a tendency to overestimate. In the case of emerging markets, its estimate rounded to 0.7 of 1 percent. The LMT errors either rounded to zero or were negative, indicating a tendency to underestimate. In the cases of small-cap stocks and emerging markets, LMT underestimated by 0.7 and 0.8 of 1 percent, respectively. For the series in Table 3.1, then, LMT was the least successful and NLN the second least successful method of approximation.

RELATIONSHIPS AMONG APPROXIMATION METHODS

For all series reported in Table 3.1, the approximations were ordered as follows:

$$g_{\text{NLN}} \geq g_{\text{QE}} \geq g_{\text{HL}} \geq g_{\text{EDD}} \geq g_{\text{LMT}} \tag{12}$$

In this section, we will show that the first two of these inequalities, namely,

$$g_{\text{MLN}} \geq g_{\text{QE}} \geq g_{\text{HL}}$$

is a mathematical relationship that is true for any return distribution with a finite variance (and therefore a finite mean as well). The inequalities are "strong" ($>$) unless the distribution has zero variance, in which case the three estimates are the same. We will also show that a third inequality

$$g_{HL} \geq g_{EDD}$$

is true as long as the expected return E and standard deviation σ of the return distribution in questions satisfy (approximately)

$$\sigma < 0.93(1 + E)$$

This condition is easily met even by the wildest of the distributions in either of our databases. Finally, we show that the fourth inequality

$$g_{EDD} \geq g_{LMT}$$

is not to be expected in general (in fact, it is violated by three of the distributions in our DMS sample).

The remainder of the present section derives the relationships just discussed. The following section reports the efficacy of the five approximations (other than Q0) for the DMS database.

To establish the relationships just asserted, it will be useful to express each function in Equations (10) (other than g_{Q0}) as an approximation to $\log[(1 + g)/(1 + E)]$. From their definitions, one can derive

$$\log[(1 + g_{QE})/(1 + E)] = -\frac{1}{2}V/(1 + E)^2 \qquad (13a)$$

$$\log[(1 + g_{\text{EDD}})/(1 + E)] = -\frac{1}{2}V/(1 + E)^2 - \frac{3}{4}V^2/(1 + E)^4 \quad \textbf{(13b)}$$

$$\log[(1 + g_{\text{LMT}})/(1 + E)] = \log\left[1 - \frac{1}{2}V/(1 + E)\right] \quad \textbf{(13c)}$$

$$\log[(1 + g_{\text{NLN}})/(1 + E)] = -\frac{1}{2}\log[1 + V/(1 + E)^2] \quad \textbf{(13d)}$$

$$\log[(1 + g_{\text{HL}})/(1 + E)] = \frac{1}{2}\log[1 - V/(1 + E)^2] \quad \textbf{(13e)}$$

With the exception of g_{LMT}, the expressions on the right of Equations (13a) through (13e) depend only on

$$X = \sigma/(1 + E) \quad \textbf{(14a)}$$

or, more directly, on its square:

$$Y = X^2 \quad \textbf{(14b)}$$
$$= V/(1 + E)^2$$

On the other hand, g_{LMT} depends on

$$\tilde{X} = \sigma/\sqrt{1 + E} \quad \textbf{(14c)}$$

or, more directly, on

$$\tilde{Y} = \tilde{X}^2 \quad \textbf{(14d)}$$
$$= V/(1 + E)$$

We know that g_{NLN} is exactly right if the return distribution is lognormal and that g_{HL} is exactly right for distributions with two equally likely outcomes. Since these two scale according to X in Equation (14a) rather than $\tilde{X}$ in Equation (14c), as does g_{QE} based on the Taylor series approximation around $R = E$, it seems that approximating

$$(1 + g)/(1 + E)$$

as a function $\sigma/(1 + E)$ is to be preferred to approximating it as a function $\sigma/\sqrt{1 + E}$. It seems plausible, then, to seek a preferred approximation method among QE, EDD, NLN, and HL—ignoring LMT. On the other hand, since the latter is so convenient for back-of-the-envelope calculations, we will examine the relationship of LMT to the other methods after we examine the relationships among QE, EDD, NLN, and HL themselves.

With Y as defined in Equation (14b), we can express the formulas in Equations (13a), (13b), (13d), and (13e) as

$$\log[(1 + g_{QE})/(1 + E)] = -\frac{1}{2}Y \tag{15a}$$

$$\log[(1 + g_{EDD})/(1 + E)] = -\frac{1}{2}Y - \frac{3}{4}Y^2 \tag{15b}$$

$$\log[(1 + g_{NLN})/(1 + E)] = -\frac{1}{2}\log(1 + Y) \tag{15c}$$

$$\log[(1 + g_{HL})/(1 + E)] = \frac{1}{2}\log(1 - Y) \tag{15d}$$

Obviously

$$g_{QE} \geq g_{EDD} \qquad (16a)$$

where equality holds only if $Y = 0$; therefore, $\sigma = 0$. Since $-\log(1 + Y)$ is convex and $\log(1 - Y)$ is concave, Y is nonnegative, and since Y, $-\log(1 + Y)$, and $\log(1 - Y)$ have the same values, and values of their first derivatives, at $Y = 0$, it follows that

$$-\log(1 + Y) \geq Y \geq \log(1 + Y)$$

where the equality holds only for $Y = 0$. This, in turn, implies

$$g_{NLN} \geq g_{QE} \geq g_{HL} \qquad (16b)$$

where the equality holds only if $\sigma = 0$.

Figure 3.2 shows QE, EDD, NLN, and HL plotted against $X = \sigma/(1 + E)$. Inequalities (16) settle all questions of the order among the four measures that depend on X, except whether HL is always greater than EDD, as in Figure 3.1, or is sometimes below it. We see in Figure 3.2 that g_{HL} crosses g_{EDD} when $X = \sigma/(1 + E)$ equals 0.93, rounded to two places. Since the largest value of X among the series in Tables 3.1 and 3.4 is emerging markets with $X = 0.31$, it seems safe to assume that, in practice, portfolios whose g are to be estimated will have $X \ll 0.93$. Therefore, for all relevant situations, the ranking of the four approximations is

$$g_{NLN} > g_{QE} > g_{HL} > g_{EDD} \qquad (17)$$

FIGURE 3.2 $(1 + g)/(1 + E)$ for Various MV Approximations as a Function of Standard Deviation/$(1 + E)$.

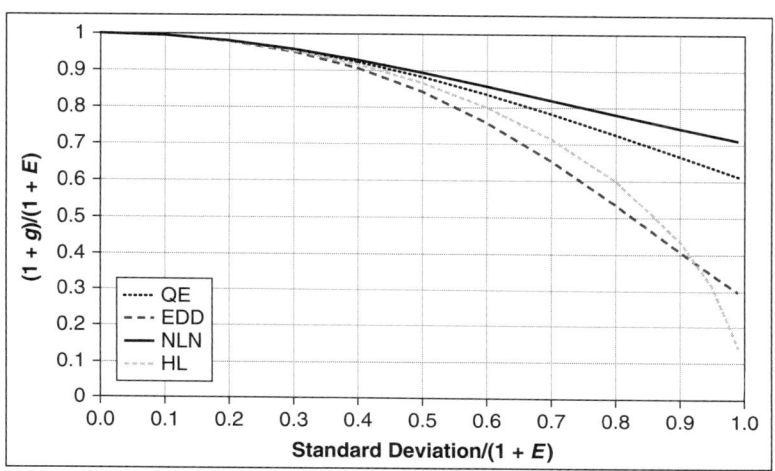

We cannot plot the LMT approximation in Figure 3.2 because its value of $(1 + g)/(1 + E)$ is a function of $\tilde{X}$ in Equation (14c) rather than X in (14a). Figure 3.3 shows how LMT compares with the other approximations as E varies, for fixed σ. Specifically, the figure shows

$$E - (\text{approx. to } g)$$

for the five approximations to g as a function of E with σ fixed at 0.2. For LMT, the difference is a constant, since

$$E - \text{LMT} = E - \left(E - \frac{1}{2}V\right) \quad (18a)$$

$$= \frac{1}{2}V$$

96 • Risk-Return Analysis

In contrast,

$$\lim_{E \to \infty}(E - \text{approx. to } g) = 0 \tag{18b}$$

for the four other approximation methods.[4]

As Figure 3.3 illustrates, at $E = 0$, LMT subtracts more from E to approximate g than do NLN and QE and less than HL and EDD; therefore, LMT supplies a lower approximation than the former two and a higher approximation than the latter two. As E falls below zero, the four approximations that depend directly on $\sigma/(1 + E)$ subtract increasing amounts. For $E < -0.05$ in particular, LMT is greater than any of the other approximations. For $E > 0.05$, on the other hand, LMT is less than the others. Finally, if the Y-dependent

FIGURE 3.3 *E* Approximation as a Function of *E* for Various Approximation Methods with Standard Deviation = 0.2.

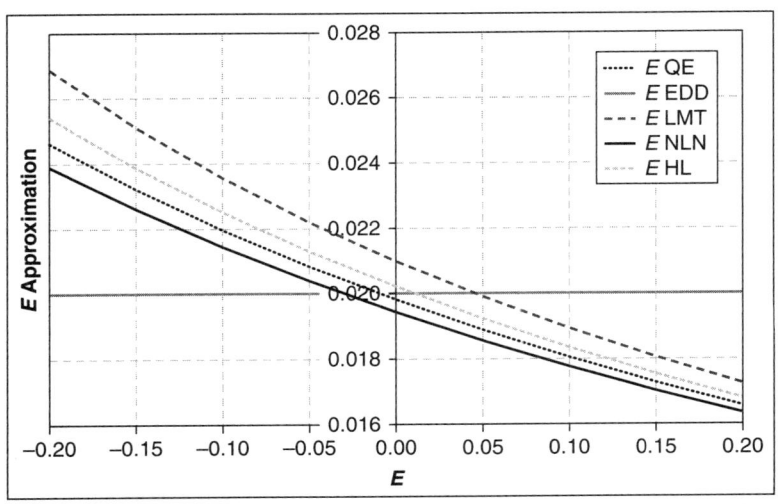

approximations bracket the true g, then the g_{LMT} back-of-the-envelope approximation substantially underestimates g for "interesting" levels of E, that is, for $E > 0.05$.

TWENTIETH-CENTURY REAL EQUITY RETURNS

Table 3.4 and Figure 3.4 show the same information for 16 countries during the twentieth century that Table 3.1 and Figure 3.1 show for commonly used asset classes. At first glance, it might seem that some series in Figure 3.4 violate the analytically established bounds on the spread among estimates illustrated in Figure 3.2. This is because of series in the figure with the same, or almost the same, standard deviations. In particular, as we can see more clearly in Table 3.5, Figure 3.4 includes series with standard deviations equal to 20.0, 20.1, and 20.2, and three series with standard deviations equal to 22.8. This source of confusion is analyzed in Table 3.5, which is organized like Table 3.2. In particular, we see in Table 3.5 that the three series with standard deviations equal to 20.0 through 20.2 have ranges equal to 0.188, 0.168, and 0.211, respectively. Each of these rounds to a range of 0.2 of 1 percent. But the three series together include a low of −0.42 and a high of 0.17, which may appear in Figure 3.4 as a range of 0.59. Thus when comparing Figure 3.4 with Figure 3.1 visually, it is best to ignore the three series with standard deviations between 20.0 and 20.2 and the three with standard deviations equal to 22.8.

Figure 3.1 includes four fixed-income series plus an inflation series, all with standard deviations less than 10 percent, as

TABLE 3.4 Geometric Mean Approximations to Various International Real Return Indices

Series	Arith. Mean.	Std. Dev.	Geom. Mean	Q0	QE	EDD	LMT	NLN	HL	Q0 Error	QE Error	EDD Error	LMT Error	NLN Error	HL Error
Australia	9.0	17.7	7.5	7.3	7.6	7.5	7.4	7.6	7.6	−0.2	0.1	0.0	−0.1	0.1	0.1
Belgium	4.8	22.8	2.5	2.1	2.3	2.2	2.2	2.4	2.3	−0.4	−0.2	−0.3	−0.3	−0.1	−0.2
Canada	7.7	16.8	6.4	6.2	6.4	6.4	6.3	6.4	6.4	−0.2	0.0	0.0	−0.1	0.0	0.0
Denmark	6.2	20.1	4.6	4.1	4.3	4.2	4.2	4.3	4.3	−0.5	−0.3	−0.4	−0.4	−0.3	−0.3
France	6.3	23.1	3.8	3.5	3.8	3.6	3.6	3.9	3.8	−0.3	0.0	−0.2	−0.2	0.1	0.0
Germany	8.8	32.3	3.6	3.2	4.1	3.5	3.6	4.3	3.9	−0.4	0.5	−0.1	0.0	0.7	0.3
Ireland	7.0	22.2	4.8	4.4	4.7	4.6	4.5	4.8	4.7	−0.4	−0.1	−0.2	−0.3	0.0	−0.1
Italy	6.8	29.4	2.7	2.3	2.8	2.4	2.5	3.0	2.7	−0.4	0.1	−0.3	−0.2	0.3	0.0
Japan	9.3	30.3	4.5	4.4	5.2	4.7	4.7	5.3	5.0	−0.1	0.7	0.2	0.2	0.8	0.5
Netherlands	7.7	21.0	5.8	5.3	5.7	5.6	5.5	5.7	5.6	−0.5	−0.1	−0.2	−0.3	−0.1	−0.2

South Africa	9.1	22.8	6.8	6.3	6.7	6.6	6.5	6.8	6.7	−0.5	−0.1	−0.2	−0.3	0.0	−0.1
Spain	5.8	22.0	3.6	3.3	3.5	3.4	3.4	3.6	3.5	−0.3	−0.1	−0.2	−0.2	0.0	−0.1
Sweden	9.9	22.8	7.6	7.0	7.6	7.4	7.3	7.6	7.5	−0.6	0.0	−0.2	−0.3	0.0	−0.1
Switzerland*	6.9	20.4	5.0	4.7	5.0	4.9	4.8	5.0	4.9	−0.3	0.0	−0.1	−0.2	0.0	−0.1
UK	7.6	20.0	5.8	5.5	5.8	5.7	5.6	5.8	5.7	−0.3	0.0	−0.1	−0.2	0.0	−0.1
USA	8.7	20.2	6.7	6.5	6.8	6.7	6.7	6.9	6.8	−0.2	0.1	0.0	0.0	0.2	0.1
								Average	−0.4	0.0	−0.1	−0.2	0.1	0.0
								Avg. abs.	0.4	0.2	0.2	0.2	0.2	0.1
								Max. abs.	0.6	0.7	0.4	0.4	0.8	0.5
								Number times best	1	7	3	2	10	4

Source: Dimson, Marsh, and Stauton (2002), Table 4.3, p. 60.

*Swiss Equities are from 1911

100 • Risk-Return Analysis

FIGURE 3.4 Approximation Errors versus Standard Deviation–Twentieth-Century Real Equity Market Returns.

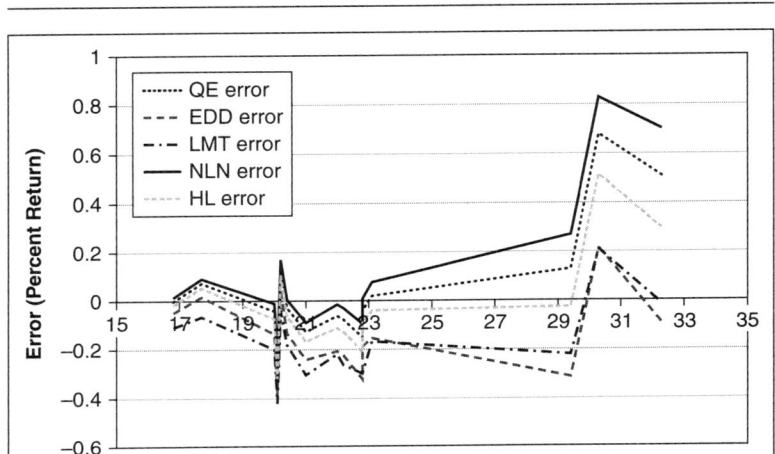

well as four equity series, all with standard deviations exceeding 20 percent. Figure 3.4 has only equity series, all with standard deviations exceeding 17 percent. Thus, it is best to ignore the series with the five lowest standard deviations in Figure 3.1 when comparing it with Figure 3.4.

In each of the four equity series in Figure 3.1, the five approximations shown in the figure bracket the actual geometric mean: The highest approximation, supplied by NLN, is always an overestimate, and the lowest approximation, supplied by LMT, is always an underestimate. The median estimate, supplied by HL, always has an absolute error that rounds to 0.2 of 1 percent or less. But it is not true of the series in Figure 3.4 that the approximations always bracket the actual geometric mean. As the "Max" column of Table 3.5 shows, in the case of

TABLE 3.5 Table 3.4 Errors, to Three Places, Sorted by Standard Deviation

Std. Dev.	QE Error	EDD Error	LMT Error	NLN Error	HL Error	Avg.	Min.	Max.	Range
16.8	−0.002	−0.050	−0.111	0.013	−0.018	−0.034	−0.111	0.013	0.124
17.7	0.072	0.016	−0.066	0.091	0.053	0.033	−0.066	0.091	0.157
20.0	−0.043	−0.137	−0.200	−0.012	−0.075	−0.093	−0.200	−0.012	0.188
20.1	−0.285	−0.386	−0.420	−0.252	−0.319	−0.333	−0.420	−0.252	0.168
20.2	0.139	0.044	−0.040	0.170	0.107	0.084	−0.040	0.170	0.211
20.4	−0.029	−0.133	−0.181	0.005	−0.065	−0.080	−0.181	0.005	0.186
21.0	−0.128	−0.243	−0.305	−0.091	−0.167	−0.187	−0.305	−0.091	0.214
22.0	−0.063	−0.208	−0.220	−0.016	−0.113	−0.124	−0.220	−0.016	0.204
22.2	−0.078	−0.224	−0.264	−0.031	−0.128	−0.145	−0.264	−0.031	0.233
22.8	−0.151	−0.323	−0.299	−0.095	−0.210	−0.216	−0.323	−0.095	0.227
22.8	−0.057	−0.209	−0.299	−0.007	−0.109	−0.136	−0.299	−0.007	0.292
22.8	−0.040	−0.189	−0.299	0.009	−0.091	−0.122	−0.299	0.009	0.308
23.1	0.019	−0.154	−0.168	0.076	−0.040	−0.053	−0.168	0.076	0.244
29.4	0.129	−0.313	−0.222	0.270	−0.026	−0.032	−0.313	0.270	0.583
30.3	0.680	0.215	0.210	0.828	0.516	0.490	0.210	0.828	0.618
32.3	0.510	−0.095	−0.016	0.701	0.295	0.279	−0.095	0.701	0.796
Avg. error	0.042	−0.149	−0.181	0.104	−0.024	−0.042	−0.181	0.104	0.285
Avg. abs.	0.152	0.184	0.208	0.167	0.146	0.171	0.146	0.208	0.062
Max. abs.	0.680	0.386	0.420	0.828	0.516	0.566	0.386	0.828	0.442

102 • Risk-Return Analysis

series with standard deviations equal to 20.0, 20.1, and 21.0, the estimate supplied by NLN is an underestimate; therefore, all the other approximation methods underestimate by even more. This is true for a total of 7 out of these 16 series.

Nevertheless, in every series, the absolute error of HL rounds at most to 0.3 of 1 percent *except* for the one with standard deviation equal to 30.3, namely, the twentieth-century stock market real returns of Japan. Another noteworthy feature of the latter series is that it is the only series in both databases in which the EDD is an *overestimate*. The difficulty with the Japan series does not lie solely in its large standard deviation, since the small-cap and EM series in Table 3.1 have larger standard deviations but were not as difficult to approximate as the Japan series. (For brevity, we will refer to a difficult-to-approximate series as *intractable*.)

Except for the Japan series, among the series in Table 3.4 and Figure 3.4, the Germany series is the most intractable. The difference between the intractability of the Germany and Japan series, on the one hand, and that of the other 14 series in Table 3.4, on the other, is analyzed in Table 3.6. Some numbers in Table 3.6 stand by themselves or *precede* a plus sign. In each column, these total to 14. The table also contains numbers that *follow* the plus sign. In any column, these total to 2. The former numbers supply the same information for the series in Table 3.4, other than Germany and Japan, as the numbers in Table 3.3 do for Table 3.1. The numbers after the plus signs present this information for the Germany and Japan series.

If we ignore Germany and Japan, the relative accuracy of the five approximations is similar to that shown in Table 3.3.

TABLE 3.6 Frequencies of Table 3.4 Errors

Abs. Error	QE	EDD	LMT	NLN	HL
0.0	5	3	1 + 1	7	3
0.1	7	2 + 1	2	4	8
0.2	1	6 + 1	5 + 1	1	2
0.3	1	2	5	2	1 + 1
0.4		1	1		
0.5	0 + 1				0 + 1
0.6					
0.7	0 + 1			0 + 1	
0.8				0 + 1	

True, HL doesn't do quite as well in Table 3.6 as in Table 3.3: In Table 3.3, seven out of nine of its absolute errors rounded to zero error, while the remaining two rounded to 0.1 and 0.2 of 1 percent. In Table 3.6, HL has zero error in three series as compared to QE and NLN, whose absolute errors rounded to zero for five and seven series, respectively. However, in Table 3.6, the absolute error of HL rounds to either 0.0 or 0.1 eleven times, which ties that of NLN and is only slightly behind that of QE at 12.

Still ignoring the Japan and Germany series, the QE, NLN, and HL approximations are clearly superior to EDD and (especially) to LMT. Only EDD and LMT have absolute errors as large as 0.4 among these numbers. EDD has an error that rounds to zero only three times, and LMT only once.

Their errors round to either 0.0 or 0.1 only 3 to 5 times as compared to 11 or 12 times for the other three methods.

In the case of Germany and Japan, in contrast, LMT adds one more to its single case that rounds to zero. The other tallies for EDD and LMT for the Japan and Germany series round to 0.1 or 0.2. For every series listed in both Tables 3.1 and 3.4 except Japan, LMT provides an underestimate, sometimes a large underestimate. Only for the Japan series does LMT overestimate g.

The reason for the varying intractability of different series is explained in part by Table 3.7. The first column of the table lists the names of six series whose relative intractability may seem puzzling. The first four series are the ones with the largest standard deviations: small-cap, emerging markets, Germany, and Japan. The last pair, Denmark and the United States, are two of those that cause confusion in Figure 3.4 because they have similar standard deviations, namely 20.1 and 20.2, respectively, but perceptibly different ranges of misestimates. The first (Denmark) is associated with *underestimates* only, of either −0.3 and −0.4 of 1 percent, whereas the second (the United States) has *overestimates* that range from 0.0 to 0.2 when rounded.

The second column of Table 3.7 lists the arithmetic mean of the series; the third column lists its maximum loss. The next column has $\log(1 + R)$ for R equal to maximum loss. The following one has the QE approximation to $\log(1 + R)$ in Equation (11b). We use the QE approximation to $\log(1 + R)$ for two reasons. First, it is one of the four approximations

TABLE 3.7 Errors in QE Approximation at Extreme Returns for Various Return Series

Series	Arith. Mean	Max. Loss	Ln(1 + r)	QE Approx.	Error	Max. Gain	Ln(1 + r)	QE Approx.	Error	Contr. to Ln Error	Actual Ln Error	N
Small cap	0.166	−0.580	−0.868	−0.691	0.177	1.429	0.887	0.650	−0.237	−0.0007	0.0018	85
EM	0.200	−0.532	−0.759	−0.614	0.146	0.559	0.444	0.437	−0.007	0.0060	0.0048	23
Germany	0.088	−0.896	−2.263	−1.229	1.034	1.559	0.940	0.522	−0.417	0.0061	0.0051	101
Japan	0.093	−0.840	−1.833	−1.129	0.704	1.196	0.787	0.589	−0.198	0.0050	0.0068	101
Denmark	0.062	−0.284	−0.334	−0.319	0.015	1.061	0.723	0.558	−0.165	−0.0015	−0.0029	101
U.S.	0.087	−0.380	−0.478	−0.438	0.040	0.568	0.450	0.428	−0.022	0.0002	0.0014	101

that is a function of $\sigma/(1 + E)$, and is in fact an inner one, providing neither the highest nor the lowest estimate for each series. Second, and equally important, the error made by QE in estimating $\log(1 + g) = E \log(1 + R)$ may be expressed as the average of individual errors $Q(R_t) - \log(1 + R_t)$, where $Q(\ )$ is the quadratic on the right-hand side of Equation (11b). This allows us to determine the contribution to the total error made by specific observations. The sixth column shows the error at R equal to maximum loss. The seventh column shows the maximum gain of the series, and the following three columns show $\log(1 + R)$, $Q(R)$, and $Q(R) - \log(1 + R)$ for maximum gain.

The third from the last column shows the contribution to the total error from the largest loss and largest gain, taken together, obtained by adding their errors and dividing by sample size (last column). This does not constitute the entire actual error (shown in the next-to-last column), since there are up to 99 other observations entering the actual error. On the other hand, this "outliers contribution" is fairly well correlated with the total error, as may be seen in Figure 3.5. The figure's horizontal axis is the contribution made by the outliers, while the vertical axis shows the actual value of total error. The straight line is the 45-degree ($Y = X$) line; the broken line connects the observed combinations of total error versus outliers contribution.

It turns out that Japan—with an outliers contribution that rounds to 0.005 and an actual error that rounds to 0.007—is somewhat anomalous even in present terms when

FIGURE 3.5 Actual Error versus Extremes Contribution.

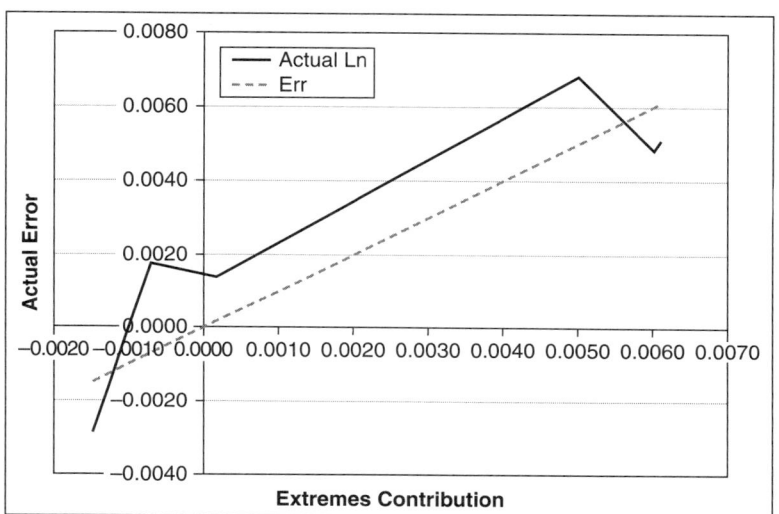

compared to the emerging markets and Germany series, whose outlier contributions are each 0.006, whereas their actual errors round to 0.005. However, the figure does distinguish clearly between these and small cap with a high standard deviation but an outliers contribution of −0.001 and a total error of 0.002. The analysis also gets the correct direction in explaining the difference between Denmark (with an outliers contribution of −0.001 versus an actual error of −0.003) and the United States (with an outliers contribution of 0.000 and an actual error of 0.001).

Granted that this is not the complete explanation of the total error, let us nevertheless consider the reason why series have a larger or smaller outliers contribution. As a specific example, compare the small-cap and emerging markets rows of Table 3.7. Small cap has a greater maximum loss than emerging markets, and also a greater maximum gain, but it has a smaller outliers contribution as well as a smaller total error. Thus the *absolute values* of the errors made by the outliers, added together, do not explain the outliers contribution.

The maximum-loss observation always has a QE approximation that overestimates $\log(1 + R)$ and therefore contributes a positive error, whereas the maximum-gain observation has a QE approximation that underestimates $\log(1 + R)$, and therefore contributes a negative error. The positive error plus the negative error of the small-cap series, divided by its sample size, is smaller than that of emerging markets. Lest you think that this is due to the smaller sample size of the emerging markets series as compared to the small-cap series, note that the outliers contribution of small cap is also smaller than that of Germany and Japan, which have larger sample sizes.

To zoom in on what is going on here, note that—as far as the maximum-loss and maximum-gain years are concerned—the small-cap historical return distribution is skewed to the right much more than the emerging markets, Germany, or Japan return series. For example, the small-cap historical distribution ranges from a 58 percent loss to a 143 percent gain, whereas the EM return series ranges from a 53 percent loss to a 56 percent gain, the Germany series ranges from a 90 percent loss (!) to a 156 percent gain, and the Japan series ranges from an 84 percent loss to a 120 percent gain.

If it seems that the Germany series, with its maximum loss of 90 percent and maximum gain of 156 percent, is almost as skewed to the right as the small-cap series, with its maximum loss of 58 percent and its maximum gain of 143 percent, consider Table 3.8 and Figure 3.6, which show the gain required to have QE's gain and loss errors cancel. For example, if $R = 0.0$—which is 0.1 below the assumed $E = 0.1$—then the offsetting gain is 0.205, which is 0.105 above the E. If $R = -0.3$—which is 0.4 below E—then the offsetting gain is 0.59, which is 0.49 above the assumed E, whereas for $R = -0.9$—which is 1.00 below E—the offsetting gain is about 2.28, which is 2.18 above E.

TABLE 3.8 Gain Required to Offset QE Error from Loss (Assumes $E = 0.1$)

Abs. Loss	Gain Required
0.000	0.205
0.100	0.320
0.200	0.448
0.300	0.590
0.400	0.752
0.500	0.936
0.600	1.154
0.700	1.418
0.800	1.763
0.900	2.281

FIGURE 3.6 Gain Required to Offset QE Error from Loss, $E = 0.1$.

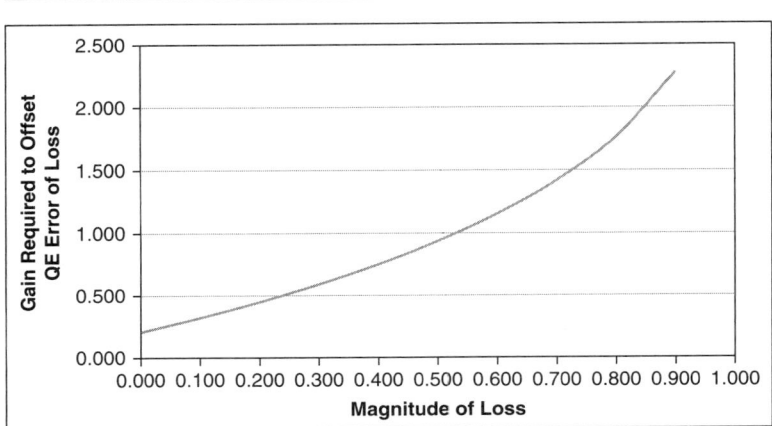

It is sometimes said that mean-variance analysis is applicable only for symmetric return distributions.[5] To the contrary, we have already seen that even the Q0 approximation, and a fortiori the QE approximation, works quite well when the return distribution is not spread out "too much," no matter what the shape of the distribution, as Markowitz (1959) noted. In addition, Figure 3.6 shows that the QE approximation to $E \log(1 + R)$ also works well if the return distribution is suitably skewed to the right, even if it is quite spread out. A particular skewed-to-the-right distribution is the lognormal, which is symmetric in the logs; that is, its probability density of $[\log(1 + R) - E \log(1 + R)]$ equals that of $-[\log(1 + R) - E \log(1 + R)]$. If return R is lognormally distributed, then the error in NLN is zero, no matter how spread out the distribution. In this case QE, HD, and

EDD would underestimate, but QE perhaps not too badly, according to Figure 3.2.

CHOICE OF APPROXIMATION

We started with six formulas for approximating g. Q0 was eliminated first. The poor performance of LMT, and the problems with it discussed in the section "Relationships Among Approximation Methods," makes its elimination a clear choice. We now consider the merits of the four remaining methods, namely, QE, EDD, NLN, and HL.

Why does EDD usually underestimate g? As previously discussed, series with low standard deviations have estimates all of which are close to one another, and therefore they usually either all overestimate or all underestimate. This is the case for the series in Figure 3.1 with $\sigma < 10$ percent and for most of the series in Figure 3.4 with $\sigma < 23$ percent. For larger standard deviations than these, except for EAFE with a standard deviation of 23.1 percent in Figure 3.1 and Japan in Figure 3.4, EDD always provides an underestimate of g. Is this just a peculiarity of the two databases examined, or is there a reason to expect EDD to usually underestimate?

To a certain degree, EDD is related to the normal distribution as NLN is related to the lognormal. NLN answers the question, "For a given E and V, what would g be if the returns were generated by a lognormal distribution?" EDD doesn't answer quite the same kind of question. Rather, it tells what the Taylor fourth-degree approximation would equal (for a given E and V) if the return distribution had the same first four moments as a normal distribution. Since the normal distribution is symmetric, the third moment makes no contribution to the approximation—as compared to the positive contribution it would make for a distribution that was skewed to the right. The contribution of the fourth moment to the approximation must necessarily be negative, as shown in Equation (13b); therefore, its inclusion reduces the estimate as compared with QE in Equation (13a).

If a Taylor approximation to the fourth degree is better than one to the second degree—assuming that the higher central moments are related to variance as in a normal distribution—what about a sixth-degree, eighth-degree, or $2n^{th}$-degree for large-n approximation on the same basis? Since all odd central moments are zero, whereas even moments are positive but have a negative weight in the Taylor expansion of the logarithm, each increase in n would further reduce the estimate. Carrying this argument to its limit, best of all would be to assume that returns are normally distributed. But since every normally distributed random variable has a positive probability that $1 + R < 0$, we would have $g = -1$ no matter that its E and $V > 0$. This would provide the maximum possible underestimate of g for all series and return distributions.

Granted that EDD does not go far down this slippery slope, the fact that the presumed rationale for EDD—pushed to the limit—produces an absurdity, plus the fact that it underestimates so frequently in these databases, plus the desirability of pruning our list of candidate approximation methods where plausible makes the deletion of EDD from the list seem, to us at least, irresistible.

The Final Three

We started with six methods for approximating the geometric mean of a series or portfolio as a function of its arithmetic mean and variance. We have eliminated three of these based on a combination of theoretical and empirical reasons. We will argue that each of the remaining three methods of approximation has at least one strong reason for not being deleted from the list; that sometimes one will be preferable and sometimes another; and that the highest and lowest may be used when a range of estimates is permitted.

Continuous financial models, such as that of Black-Scholes, frequently assume that stock prices (or indices) follow a geometric Brownian motion; that is, price or index increments are lognormally distributed, with those of nonoverlapping intervals being distributed independently. Empirically, Table 3.6 shows that the error made by NLN in the Table 3.4 database rounded to zero more often than that of any other method. Thus, if one of the final three approximations needs to be deleted, it should not be NLN.

But Table 3.3 shows that HL's errors rounded to zero most frequently in the database of Table 3.1, and Table 3.6 shows that its errors rounded to either 0 or 0.1 eleven times in the database of Table 3.4, just as NLN did. So it doesn't seem reasonable to delete HL. Finally, since QE necessarily falls between HL and NLN, it is the obvious "compromise choice" if a range of estimates is not permitted.

Choice Among Final Three

Thus the three methods of approximation—HL, QE, and NLN—should stay in our kit bag, and, where appropriate, a range of estimates should be supplied. But what if a range of estimates is not appropriate? In particular, an investor can have only one asset-class mix for his or her portfolio as a whole. Suppose he or she would like to plan for the long run by choosing the mix that maximizes g. Should the investor's advisor recommend the method that maximizes NLN, QE, or HL? Or perhaps a weighted average of these?

Our recommendation regarding these questions depends on how much the investor's advisor knows, or is willing to assume, concerning the return distribution. We distinguish four levels of knowledge or assumption:

1. The investor's advisor is willing to assume a given shape of the distribution (for example, its skewness and kurtosis in some sense), but not its location and scale.
2. The advisor is *not* willing to assume that the return distribution is of a specific shape, but *is* willing to assume that it is one of several shapes.
3. The advisor is not willing to assume that the return distribution has one of several shapes, as in (2), but is

willing to assume certain relevant properties for the return distribution.
4. The advisor knows nothing and is not willing to assume anything.

Recommendations in each of these cases follows:

1. Suppose, for example, that the advisor assumes that

$$M_3 = k_1 \sigma^3 \tag{19a}$$
$$M_4 = k_1 \sigma^4$$
$$= k_2 V^2 \tag{19b}$$

where

$$M_h = E(R - E)^h$$

Given Equations (19), M_3 and M_4 are known once E and V are given. If, further, the advisor assumes that the return distribution is a member of the Pearson family—a broad class of distributions including many familiar names—then the whole distribution is known, since the specific Pearson distribution is determined uniquely by its first four moments when these are finite. The geometric mean of the distribution can then be calculated, either by formula or numerically.

Chapter 5 illustrates the use of Pearson family members as return distributions. Our focus in that chapter is on how to estimate the probability of various possible gains and losses, rather than the computation of the geometric mean, but clearly an estimate of the whole distribution can serve both purposes.

2. Suppose that the advisor is not willing to estimate a single return distribution for a given portfolio, but is willing to assign subjective probabilities to D different specific return distributions. In the appendix to this chapter, we analyze the possibility of using these D specific distributions to choose an approximation that, itself, is a weighted average of approximations. This can be formulated as a "portfolio selection" problem with average mean-square error and average absolute error as the desiderata.

3. The third situation concerns an advisor who does not assume a form of the return distribution, but instead assumes relevant properties concerning its shape. The "relevant properties" for us are its skewness and kurtosis, particularly as these relate to the sources of error in QE, as illustrated in Tables 3.7 and 3.8 and Figure 3.6. Such considerations would suggest whether QE would tend to overestimate or underestimate g, and roughly by how much. If the QE underestimate is sufficient, then the advisor

should use NLN instead of QE, and similarly should use HL in the event of a sufficient overestimate. As to how much over- or underestimate of g is enough to justify the switch away from QE, this depends on the difference—NLN − QE or QE − HL, as appropriate—which depends on $\sigma/(1 + E)$, as illustrated in Figure 3.2.

4. If the advisor knows nothing and assumes nothing, then we recommend that the advisor stick with the middle ground, QE.

RECAP

The inputs into, and outputs from, a mean-variance efficient set computation must, of necessity, include arithmetic rather than geometric means. But the investor should be informed of the portfolio's geometric mean, since this is the portfolio's likely return in the long run. This chapter analyzed the accuracy of six methods of approximating the geometric means from the arithmetic means and variances of the series in two databases. Three of the proposed methods are discarded for a combination of theoretical and empirical reasons. In particular, the frequently used back-of-the-envelope rule—that the geometric mean is approximately the arithmetic mean minus half the variance—is likely to be misleading as an approximation to annual portfolio returns. The remaining three (the "near lognormal," the quadratic approximation about $R = E$, and the Henry Latané approximation) must necessarily satisfy

$$g_{\text{NLN}} \geq g_{\text{QE}} \geq g_{\text{HL}}$$

where equality holds only if variance is zero. One database favors g_{NLN}, another favors g_{HL}, and g_{QE} is a good compromise candidate in any case.

The next chapter considers the efficacy of risk-return approximations to g or, equivalently, $E \log(1 + r)$ using risk measures other than variance.

✳ ✳ ✳ ✳

TECHNICAL NOTE: SELECTING A WEIGHTED AVERAGE OF APPROXIMATIONS

As in the text, we assume that the advisor has selected D representative distributions, perhaps randomly from some large class of distributions. The advisor need not assume that all D distributions are equally plausible. Specifically, we will let

$$p_d, \quad d = 1, \ldots, D$$

be the probability that the advisor assigns to the statement "the geometric mean of the subject distribution bears the same relationship to its arithmetic mean and standard deviation as does the dth representative distribution." Let M be the number of methods of approximation to be considered, and let

$$w_m, \quad m = 1, \ldots, M$$

be the weights (to be determined) to be assigned to each of the M methods, forming a weighted-average estimate. Thus

$$\sum_{m=1}^{M} w_m = 1 \qquad \text{(A1a)}$$

$$w_m \geq 0, \quad m = 1, \ldots, M \qquad \text{(A1b)}$$

The w_m are required to obey inequalities (A1b), since one does not want to "short" any method. If a method should be bet against, then its negative or inverse should be used instead. Equation (A1a) is required, since if any approximation systematically over- or underestimates g, so that we should let its weight be other than 1.0 if it were the only method used, then its calculation should be adjusted accordingly. [If Equation (A1a) were omitted, then $w_m = 0$, for all m, would be the only efficient combination for the problem posed here.]

The error that a weighted average would make when applied to distribution d is

$$E_d = \sum_{m=1}^{M} w_m e_{md} \qquad \text{(A2)}$$

where e_{md} is the error from method m applied to distribution d. One can divide E_d into its positive part P_d and its negative part N_d as

$$E_d = P_d - N_d \qquad \text{(A3a)}$$

where

$$P_d \geq 0, N_d \geq 0 \qquad \text{(A3b)}$$

The optimization process defined here will ensure that either $P_d = 0$ or $N_d = 0$. We wish to make small the expected absolute error

$$A = \sum_d p_d (P_d + N_d) \qquad \text{(A4a)}$$

which is equivalent to making large

$$E = -\sum_d p_d (P_d + N_d) \qquad \text{(A4b)}$$

We also would like to make small the expected mean square error

$$S = \sum_d p_d (P_d^2 + N_d^2) \qquad \text{(A5)}$$

In other words, we seek a combination of weights $w_1, \ldots, w_M$ that is efficient in terms of E and S subject to Equations (A1a),

(A2), and (A3a) and Inequalities (A1b) and (A3b), where E and S are defined by Equations (A4a) and (A4b).

Since E is linear, S is a positive semidefinite quadratic, and the constraints are linear equality and (weak) inequality constraints, the problem of finding E, S efficient $(w_1, \ldots, w_M)$ vectors can be set up as an instance of the General Portfolio Selection Problem of Markowitz (1959), Chapter 8 and Appendix A, or Markowitz and Todd (2000). The "critical line method" presented in these references can be used to trace out the entire piecewise linear set of efficient weights in about the time it takes to obtain two or three points from this efficient frontier using a general-purpose quadratic programming algorithm.

4

ALTERNATIVE MEASURES OF RISK

INTRODUCTION

Chapter 3 compared alternative mean-variance approximations to the geometric mean or, equivalently, the expected log. The present chapter compares the QE approximation of the preceding chapter with risk-return approximations to the expected log using four alternative measures of risk. Each of these alternative risk measures has active proponents. Ideally, such proponents should either explain why expected utility should not be the touchstone of rational decision making or demonstrate that their proposed risk measure is better able to approximate expected utility than variance is. Since this has not been forthcoming from such sources, we will do our best to objectively evaluate mean-variance approximations versus approximations based on the mean and the most frequently proposed alternative measures of risk.

The risk measures to be considered in this chapter are:

Variance (V)
Mean absolute deviation (MAD)
Semivariance (SV)[1]
Value at risk (VaR)
Conditional value at risk (CVaR)

These are defined as follows:

$$\text{MAD} = E|R - E(R)|$$
$$\text{SV} = E\{\text{Min}[0, R - E(R)]\}^2$$

VaR is the largest number such that

$$\text{Prob}(R \leq -\text{VaR}) \geq p$$
$$\text{CVaR} = E(R|R \leq -\text{VaR})$$

The tests reported below use $p = 0.05$.

Konno and Yamazaki (1991) argues for MAD for portfolio selection; Sortino and Satchell (2001) argues for semivariance, a.k.a. downside risk; see Jorion (2006) regarding VaR and Kaplan (2012), who recommends CVaR.

THE ASSET-CLASS DATABASE

Table 4.1 presents historical statistics for the asset classes that appear in Table 3.1 of Chapter 3. Some statistics reported there are repeated here; some that are of immediate interest in the

TABLE 4.1 Historical Statistics for Frequently Used Asset Classes

	Mean	Geom. Mean	Std. Dev.	MAD	Semidev.	V/2SV	Raw VaR (5%)	Interp. VaR (5%)	CVaR (5%)
Large-cap stocks	0.119	0.099	0.204	0.164	0.151	0.911	0.249	0.261	0.333
Small-cap stocks	0.167	0.121	0.326	0.246	0.217	1.130	0.367	0.378	0.468
Long-term corp. bonds	0.062	0.059	0.083	0.061	0.048	1.472	0.050	0.056	0.066
Long-term gov. bonds	0.059	0.055	0.095	0.071	0.057	1.399	0.061	0.074	0.094
Intermed.-term gov. bonds	0.055	0.054	0.057	0.044	0.033	1.497	0.013	0.017	0.026
U.S. Treasury bills	0.037	0.036	0.031	0.025	0.019	1.359	−0.001	−0.001	0.000
Inflation	0.031	0.030	0.042	0.027	0.028	1.127	0.021	0.026	0.061
EAFE	0.125	0.101	0.228	0.178	0.162	0.996	0.221	0.231	0.331
EM	0.200	0.141	0.366	0.309	0.253	1.049	0.306	0.498	0.532

present chapter are reported in the present table and not the earlier one. Specifically, the first column lists the names of the asset classes. The following columns list various statistics, including the arithmetic mean, geometric mean, standard deviation, MAD, semideviation (which is the square root of semivariance), the ratio of variance to twice semivariance, and columns we refer to as raw VaR, Interpolated VaR, and CVaR.

The semivariance of a symmetric distribution is half its variance. Thus, symmetric distributions have

$$\Psi \equiv V/2SV = 1$$

Distributions that are skewed to the right have $\Psi > 1$; those that are skewed to the left have $\Psi < 1$. If $\Psi = 1$, the distribution may or may not be symmetric, but is what we will call "skew-neutral." Table 4.1 shows that the return distributions for most of the asset classes considered here are skewed to the right. The exceptions are EAFE, which is essentially skew-neutral, and large-cap stocks, which is skewed to the left.

Raw VaR is computed as if the returns in each data series were equally likely and were the only possible returns in the population. Thus, −raw VaR at the 5 percent level is the absolute value of the largest loss such that this loss—plus all returns that are worse than it—constitutes *at least* 5 percent of the population. For a small data series, there may be a considerable gap between −raw VaR and the next lower return. Interpolated VaR assumes, instead, that the return distribution has a step-function probability density with returns uniformly distributed between −raw VaR and the next lower return. Thus, interpolated VaR is, in fact, a linear interpolation between these two values.

CVaR here equals the average return given that return equals raw VaR or worse. It seemed to us unnecessary to compute CVaR using both raw VaR and interpolated VaR, since there is a large overlap in the range of the two computations. (If proponents of CVaR feel that we did their risk measure an injustice by this decision, they are encouraged to do the computation themselves with this publicly available database.)

COMPARISONS

The approximation to $E\log(1 + R) = \log(1 + g)$ in Equation (6) of Chapter 2 may be written as

$$\log(1 + E) - \log(1 + g) = \tfrac{1}{2}V/(1 + E)^2 \qquad (1)$$

Let

$$\Delta L \equiv \log(1 + E) - \log(1 + g) \qquad (2)$$

ΔL roughly equals $E - g$, underestimating it by an amount less than $\tfrac{1}{2}(E^2 - g^2)$. In the present chapter, we evaluate approximations to ΔL based on the various measures of risk listed previously for the two databases described in the previous chapter.

Table 4.2 lists asset classes in the same order as in Table 4.1, repeats their arithmetic and geometric means, and shows their ΔL. Continuing across the table, the fourth column lists the

TABLE 4.2 Variance, Semivariance, and MAD Approximations to Geometric Mean for Frequently Used Asset Classes

Mean	Geom. Mean	Ln(1 + E) − Ln(1 + G)	Variance	Variance/(1 + E)²	MAD	MAD²	MAD²/(1 + E)²	Semivar.	Semivar./(1 + E)²
0.119	0.099	0.0182	0.0416	0.0332	0.1644	0.0270	0.0216	0.0228	0.0182
0.167	0.121	0.0409	0.1065	0.0781	0.2465	0.0607	0.0446	0.0471	0.0346
0.062	0.059	0.0029	0.0069	0.0061	0.0607	0.0037	0.0033	0.0023	0.0021
0.059	0.055	0.0038	0.0091	0.0081	0.0711	0.0051	0.0045	0.0032	0.0029
0.055	0.054	0.0014	0.0032	0.0029	0.0437	0.0019	0.0017	0.0011	0.0010
0.037	0.036	0.0004	0.0010	0.0009	0.0246	0.0006	0.0006	0.0004	0.0003
0.031	0.030	0.0008	0.0017	0.0016	0.0272	0.0007	0.0007	0.0008	0.0007
0.125	0.101	0.0216	0.0522	0.0412	0.1778	0.0316	0.0250	0.0262	0.0207
0.200	0.141	0.0504	0.1342	0.0932	0.3088	0.0953	0.0663	0.0639	0.0444
		Beta	0.38	0.53	0.15	0.58	0.82	0.82	1.13
		RMSQ%	0.10	0.05	0.51	0.29	0.20	0.11	0.12

variance, V, of each series, and the fifth lists $V/(1 + E)^2$, which we will refer to as "adjusted variance." The next three columns present MAD, MAD^2, and $MAD^2/(1 + E)^2$. We will refer to the last two as "MAD-squared" and "adjusted MAD-squared," respectively. The final two columns of Table 4.2 present the semivariance (SV) and $SV/(1 + E)^2$, which we refer to as the "adjusted semivariance."

For each function f of the risk measure RM, we fit a regression with zero intercept:

$$\Delta L = \beta \cdot f(RM) \qquad (3)$$

The fit with zero intercept is appropriate, since a series with no variability has $E = g$, and therefore $\Delta L = 0$. For a level playing field, we compare the efficacy of adjusted variance to that of the other $f(RM)$ using a fitted beta rather than the Taylor series–determined $\beta = 0.5$—though the fitted beta, $\beta = 0.53$, is close to the Taylor series beta.

For each $f(RM)$, the last two rows of Table 4.2 show its beta and its root-mean-squared error (RMSQ) as a percentage. For example, using twice RMSQ as a confidence interval, if the adjusted variance estimate of the geometric mean is 10.0 percent, this estimate is subject to an error of probably no more than $2 \cdot (0.05) = 0.10$ percent, that is, 10 bps (where a basis point, bp, is 1/100 of 1 percent). MAD, with an RMSQ = 0.51, on the other hand, is subject to an estimated error of probably no more than plus or minus 102 bps, or slightly over one percentage point. Adjusted MAD-squared does much better, with an RMSQ of 20 bps and therefore a confidence

FIGURE 4.1 Ln(1 + E) − Ln(1 + G), A + B × MAD, and Beta × MAD for Frequently Used Asset Classes.

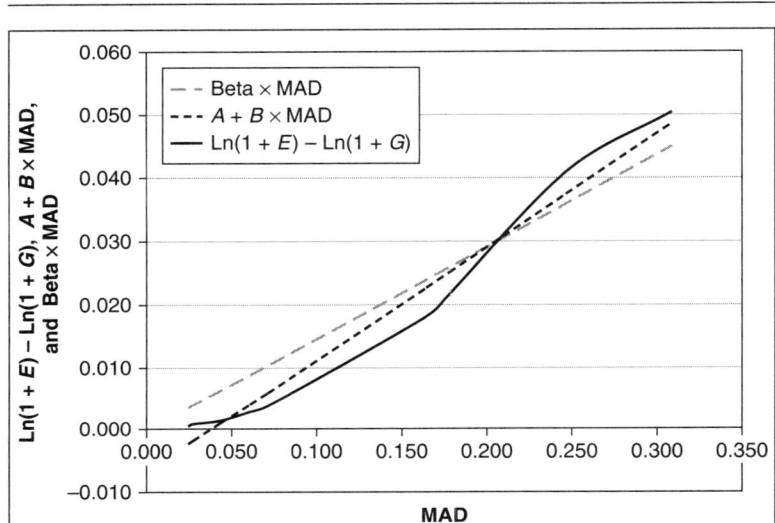

interval of ±40 bps, roughly twice that of variance and semivariance and four times that of adjusted variance.

The reason that MRSQ for MAD is so high is illustrated in Figure 4.1. The figure plots MAD on the horizontal axis and curves connecting three values of ΔL on the vertical axis. Specifically, the two straight lines are the regression of ΔL against MAD in which the intercept is allowed any value and that in which it is forced to be zero. The third curve shows the actual value of ΔL for each observation. As Figure 4.1 illustrates, the regression with an unconstrained intercept estimates a negative $\Delta L (=-0.07)$ when MAD = 0. This is not possible, since we know that E is always at least as great as g and therefore $\Delta L \geq 0$. Thus the relevant line is the one with the regression

FIGURE 4.2 Ln(1 + E) − Ln(1 + G) versus (MAD²)/(1 + E)² for Frequently Used Asset Classes.

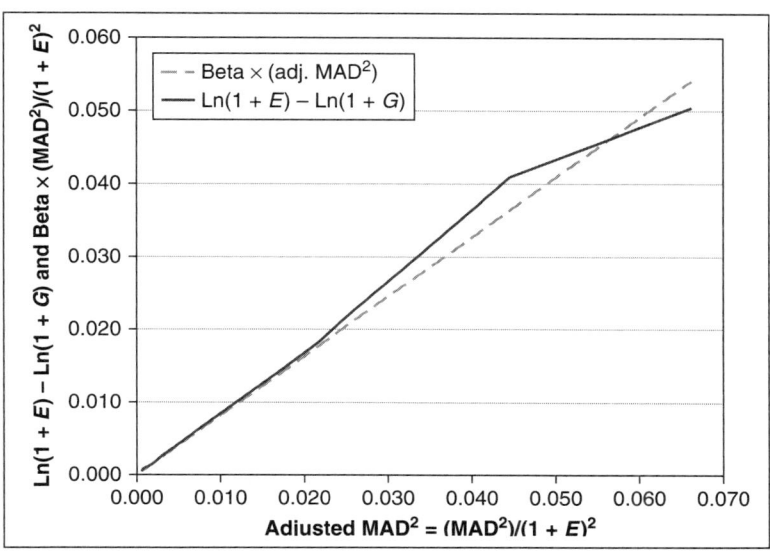

forced to go through the origin. As the figure illustrates, MAD has two problems in fitting the data. One is that its best intercept is negative, and the other is that the curve of actual ΔL versus MAD is clearly nonlinear. On the other hand, the same data for adjusted MAD-squared, presented in Figure 4.2, show the curve of actual ΔL to be much closer to linear and to almost go through the origin. This reduces RMSQ considerably, but not to that of variance, whose fit versus actual ΔL is shown in Figure 4.3, or that of adjusted variance, shown in Figure 4.4. The latter fit seems to us to be truly remarkable.

Figure 4.5 illustrates the fit to ΔL by semivariance, which, according to Table 4.2, is slightly better than that of adjusted

FIGURE 4.3 Ln(1 + E) − Ln(1 + G) versus Variance for Frequently Used Asset Classes.

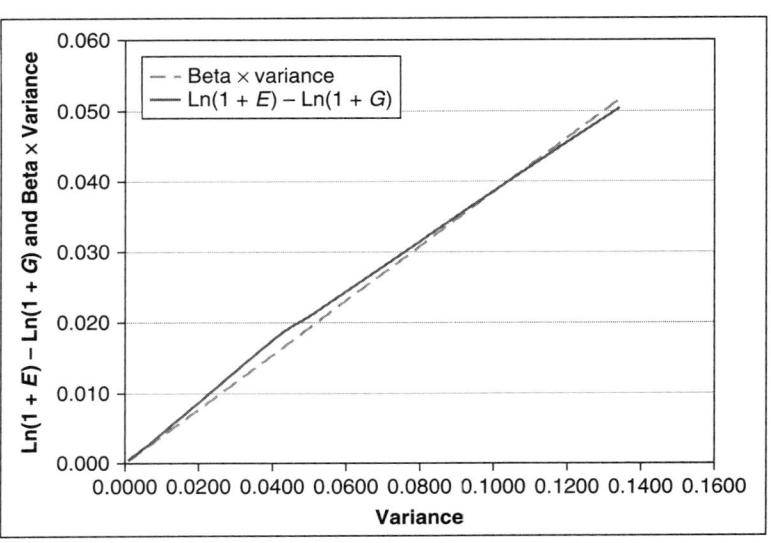

FIGURE 4.4 Ln(1 + E) − Ln(1 + G) versus Variance/(1 + E)² for Frequently Used Asset Classes.

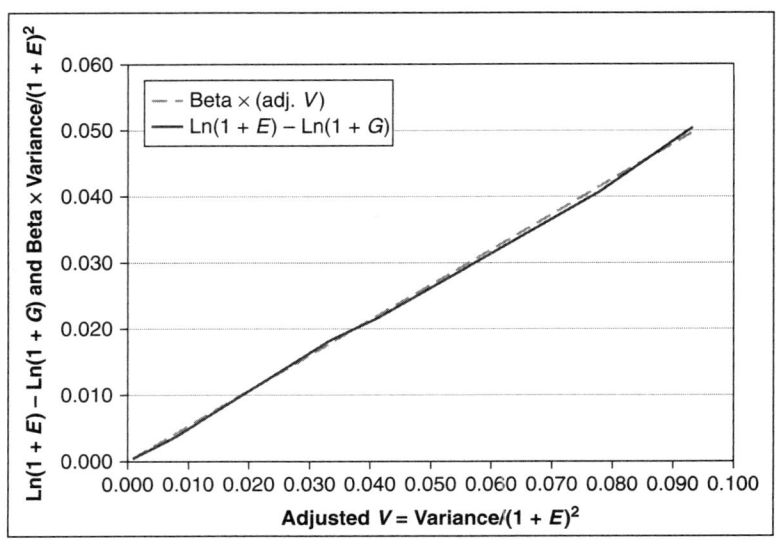

FIGURE 4.5 Ln(1 + E) − Ln(1 + G) versus Semivariance for Frequently Used Asset Classes.

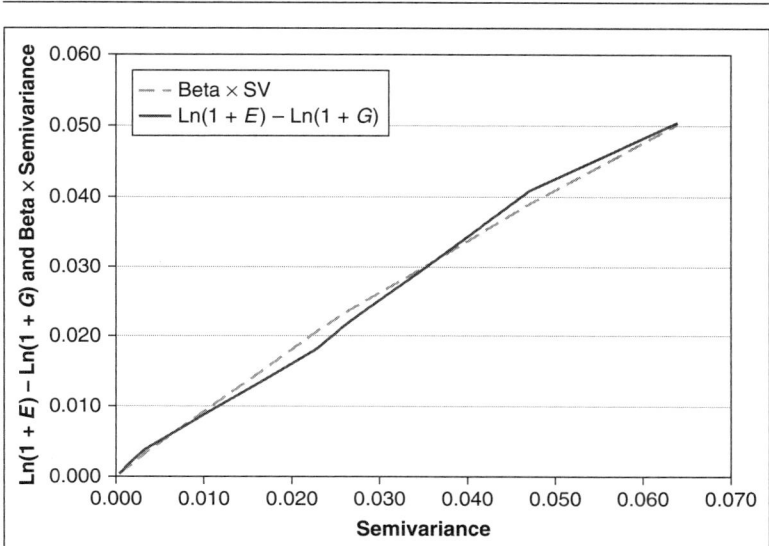

semivariance. The figure shows the actual ΔL curve for semivariance to be approximately linear and through the origin.

The first four columns of Table 4.3 repeat information for the arithmetic and geometric means, ΔL, and adjusted variance. This is followed by columns for risk measures raw VaR and the following functions of raw VaR:

$$\text{RVEV} = [(\text{raw VaR} + E)/K]^2$$

and

$$\text{Adjusted RVEV} = \{[(\text{raw VaR} + E)/K]^2\}/(1 + E)^2$$

with $K = 1.65$. RVEV stands for raw VaR estimated variance, since RVEV would equal variance for a normally distributed

TABLE 4.3 Variance, VaR, and CVaR Approximations to Geometric Mean for Frequently Used Asset Classes

Mean	Geom. Mean	Ln(1 + E) − Ln(1 + G)	$V/(1+E)^2$	Raw VaR	$[(\text{Raw VaR}+E)/K]^2$	Interp. VaR	$\{[(\text{Raw VaR}+E)/K]^2\}/(1+E)^2$	$[(\text{Interp}+E)/K]^2$	$\{[(\text{Interp. VaR}+E)/K]^2\}/(1+E)^2$	CVaR	CVaR^2	$\text{CVaR}^2/(1+E)^2$
0.119	0.099	0.0182	0.0332	0.2490	0.0497	0.0397	0.2608	0.0529	0.0423	0.3335	0.1112	0.0888
0.167	0.121	0.0409	0.0781	0.3672	0.1050	0.0770	0.3779	0.1092	0.0802	0.4680	0.2190	0.1607
0.062	0.059	0.0029	0.0061	0.0495	0.0046	0.0041	0.0556	0.0051	0.0045	0.0661	0.0044	0.0039
0.059	0.055	0.0038	0.0081	0.0609	0.0053	0.0047	0.0735	0.0064	0.0057	0.0938	0.0088	0.0079
0.055	0.054	0.0014	0.0029	0.0129	0.0017	0.0015	0.0165	0.0019	0.0017	0.0259	0.0007	0.0006
0.037	0.036	0.0004	0.0009	−0.0010	0.0005	0.0004	−0.0007	0.0005	0.0004	−0.0003	0.0000	0.0000
0.031	0.030	0.0008	0.0016	0.0208	0.0010	0.0009	0.0260	0.0012	0.0011	0.0614	0.0038	0.0036
0.125	0.101	0.0216	0.0412	0.2215	0.0442	0.0349	0.2314	0.0468	0.0369	0.3313	0.1097	0.0867
0.200	0.141	0.0504	0.0932	0.3061	0.0939	0.0653	0.4980	0.1787	0.1242	0.5318	0.2828	0.1965
	Beta	0.53	0.05	0.12	0.45	0.61	0.10	0.32	0.44	0.08	0.18	0.25
	RMSQ%	0.05	0.65	0.38	0.46	0.32	0.38	0.30	0.48	0.15	0.17	

VaR and CVaR are at the 5% level. $K = 1.65$

FIGURE 4.6 Ln(1 + E) − Ln(1 + G) versus Raw VaR Approximation for Frequently Used Asset Classes.

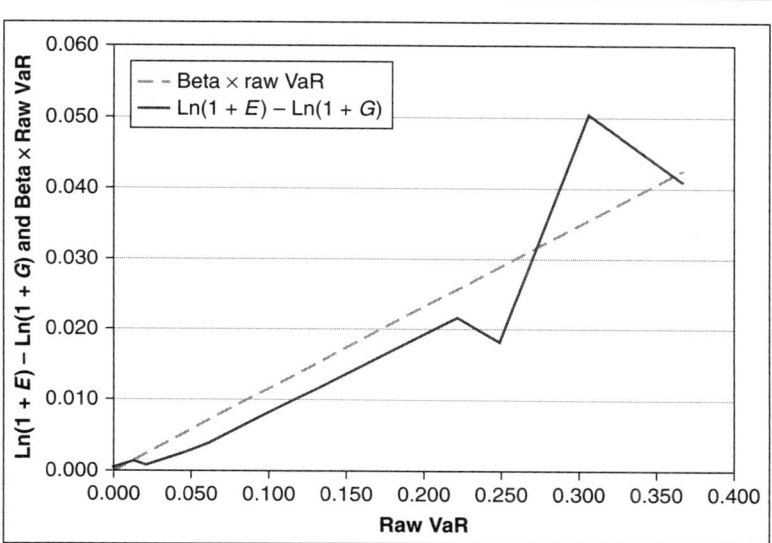

random variable with Prob($R \leq$ −raw VaR) = 0.05. RVEV does better than raw VaR itself and adjusted RVEV, but substantially worse than adjusted variance, and even worse than variance and semivariance. The fit of raw VaR and RVEV are shown in Figures 4.6 and 4.7.

The next three columns of Table 4.3 show data and results for interpolated VaR, the latter's estimated variance, and the adjusted version thereof. In this case, the adjusted version does slightly better than the plain-vanilla version. However, all versions using interpolated VaR, like all versions using raw VaR, do much worse than variance, adjusted variance, and semivariance. The actual and fit ΔL of interpolated VaR is shown in Figure 4.8.

FIGURE 4.7 Ln(1 + E) − Ln(1 + G) versus [(Raw VaR + E)/K]² for Frequently Used Asset Classes.

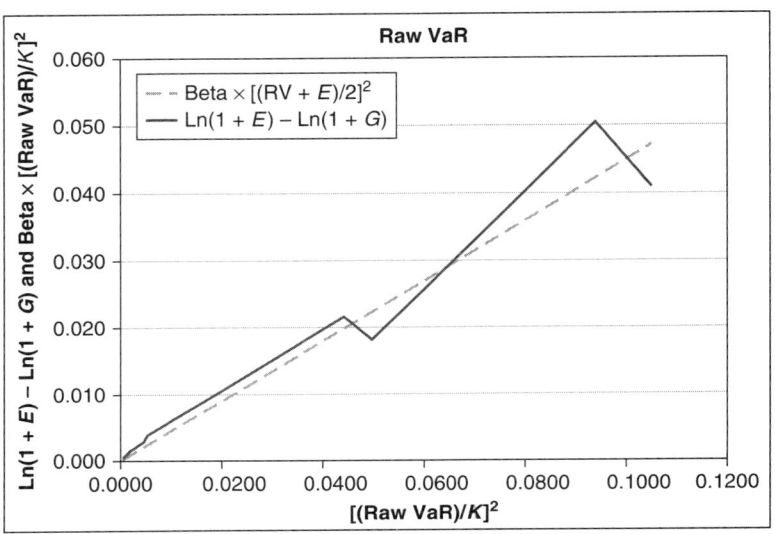

FIGURE 4.8 Ln(1 + E) − Ln(1 + G) versus Interpolated VaR for Frequently Used Asset Classes.

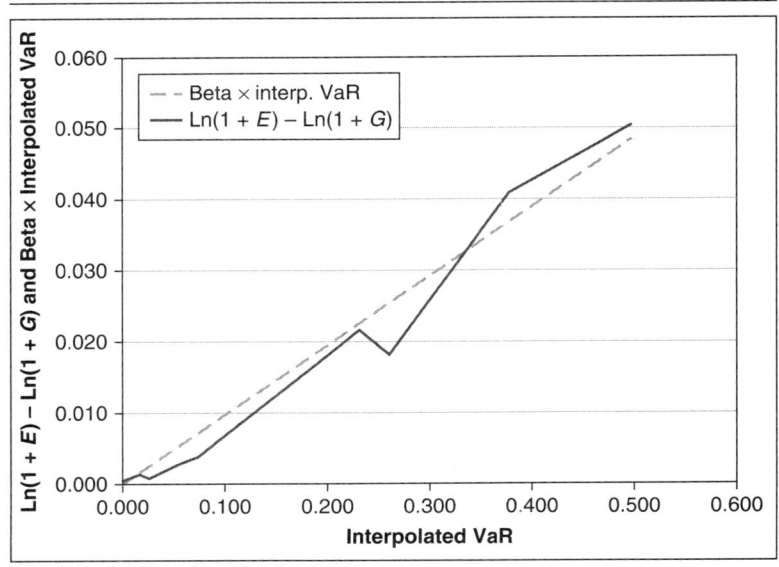

FIGURE 4.9 Ln(1 + E) − Ln(1 + G) versus CVaR for Frequently Used Asset Classes.

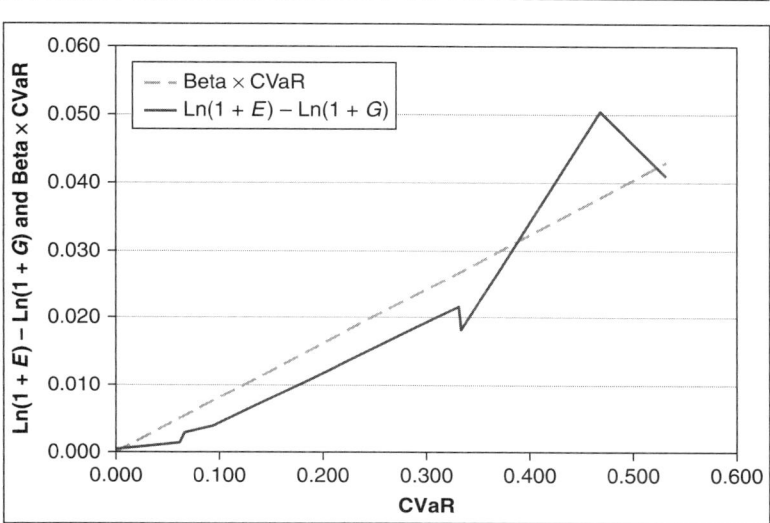

The last three columns of Table 4.3 contain CVaR, CVaR-squared, and adjusted CVaR-squared, defined like the corresponding functions of MAD. The RMSQ of CVaR-squared is slightly better than that for adjusted CVaR-squared. Both are perceptibly better than that of CVaR itself, though not quite as good as that of variance and semivariance and, a fortiori, not as good as adjusted variance. Figures 4.9 and 4.10 show the fit by CVaR and CVaR-squared.

THE DMS DATABASE

This section considers the efficacy of functions of the five risk measures against the real equity return series of the 16 countries for the twentieth century reported by DMS

FIGURE 4.10 Ln(1 + E) − Ln(1 + G) versus CVaR² for Frequently Used Asset Classes.

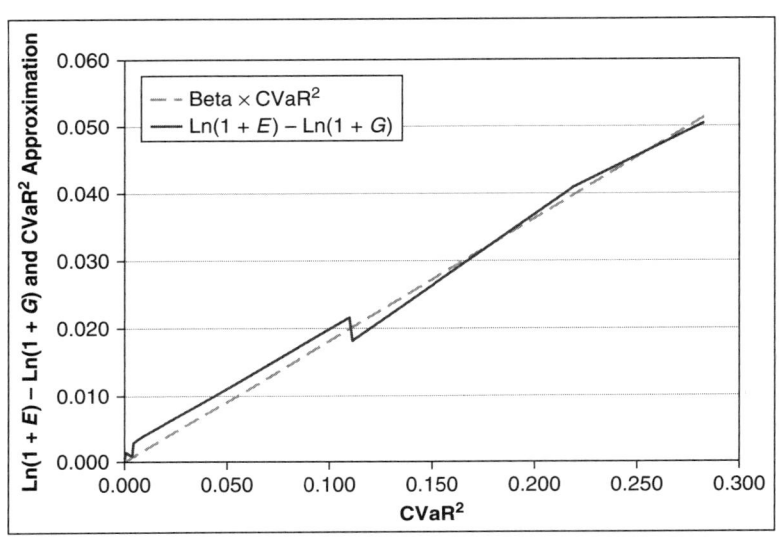

(Dimson, Marsh, and Staunton, 2002). Table 4.4 lists various statistics of these series, including their arithmetic means, geometric means, standard deviations, MADs, semideviations, $\Psi = V/2SV$, VaR, and CVaR. Since each series in this database has 101 observations, we defined VaR to be the fifth worst. Thus CVaR here is actually at the 5/1.01 percent level, and VaR = raw VaR is exactly at this level.

A principal reason that the mean-variance approximations in Chapter 3 had difficulty approximating the geometric means of some of these series was the large losses they sustained. These are shown by the bars in Figure 4.11

TABLE 4.4 Historical Statistics for 16 Equity Markets During the Twentieth Century

	Mean	Geom. Mean	Std. Dev.	MAD	Semidev.	VaR/2SV	VaR (5/1.01)%	CVaR (5/1.01)%
Australia	0.092	0.077	0.179	0.138	0.131	0.932	0.228	0.302
Belgium	0.053	0.030	0.232	0.179	0.146	1.262	0.281	0.332
Canada	0.073	0.060	0.169	0.134	0.117	1.039	0.219	0.257
Denmark	0.067	0.050	0.200	0.132	0.110	1.640	0.211	0.250
France	0.061	0.036	0.235	0.184	0.153	1.179	0.286	0.344
Germany	0.085	0.035	0.327	0.214	0.188	1.509	0.313	0.467
Ireland	0.070	0.048	0.221	0.164	0.138	1.293	0.252	0.339
Italy	0.068	0.027	0.294	0.212	0.189	1.209	0.370	0.501
Japan	0.093	0.047	0.303	0.216	0.199	1.164	0.416	0.565
Netherlands	0.077	0.059	0.211	0.153	0.129	1.337	0.203	0.277
South Africa	0.091	0.070	0.226	0.172	0.139	1.319	0.196	0.292
Spain	0.058	0.038	0.220	0.166	0.139	1.248	0.270	0.334
Sweden	0.087	0.067	0.220	0.164	0.144	1.176	0.248	0.325
Switzerland	0.065	0.047	0.195	0.143	0.128	1.153	0.251	0.299
U.K.	0.077	0.059	0.200	0.145	0.131	1.163	0.205	0.325
U.S.	0.089	0.071	0.202	0.166	0.146	0.957	0.300	0.344

in the same order as the countries listed in Table 4.4. In particular, the figure shows that six countries had maximum losses exceeding 50 percent, with three of these having maximum losses slightly exceeding 70, 80, and 90 percent, respectively.

FIGURE 4.11 Maximum Loss by 16 Equity Markets During the Twentieth Century.

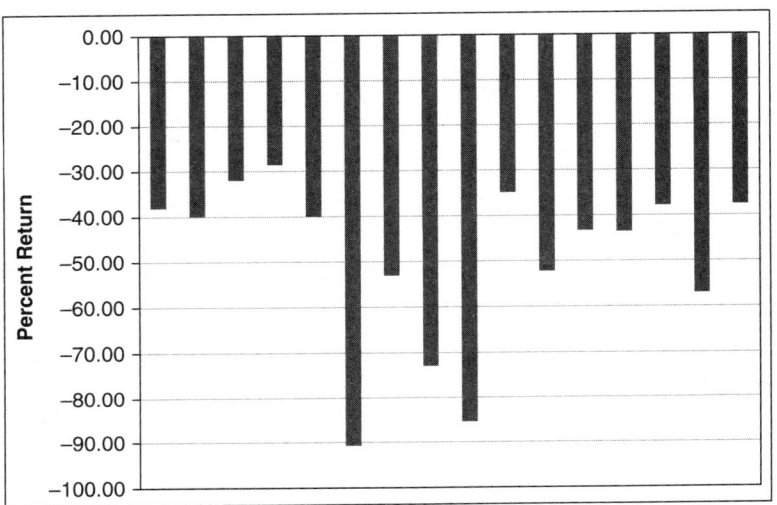

Table 4.5 has the same information for the DMS database as Table 4.2 had for asset classes. Similarly, Table 4.6 has the same information for the DMS database as Table 4.3 had. All $f(RM)$ do worse for the DMS database than they did for the asset class database. In particular, for the DMS database, variance does slightly better than adjusted variance, with RMSQs of 0.17 and 0.18, respectively. These are about half the RMSQs of semivariance and adjusted semivariance for this database. These, in turn, do slightly better than MAD-squared and adjusted MAD-squared. MAD itself does quite poorly. The best versions of VaR and CVaR have RMSQs of 0.60 and 0.46, respectively. See Figures 4.12 through 4.16.

TABLE 4.5 Variance, Semivariance, and MAD Approximations to Geometric Mean for 16 Equity Markets During the Twentieth Century

Mean	Geom. Mean	Ln(1 + E) − Ln(1 + G)	Variance	Variance/ (1 + E)²	MAD	MAD²	MAD²/ (1 + E)²	Semivar.	Semivar./ (1 + E)²
0.092	0.077	0.0134	0.0320	0.0268	0.1383	0.0191	0.0160	0.0172	0.0144
0.053	0.030	0.0226	0.0540	0.0486	0.1793	0.0322	0.0290	0.0214	0.0193
0.073	0.060	0.0124	0.0287	0.0249	0.1343	0.0180	0.0157	0.0138	0.0120
0.067	0.050	0.0160	0.0400	0.0352	0.1321	0.0175	0.0153	0.0122	0.0107
0.060	0.036	0.0237	0.0550	0.0489	0.1843	0.0340	0.0302	0.0233	0.0207
0.085	0.035	0.0470	0.1068	0.0908	0.2140	0.0458	0.0389	0.0354	0.0301
0.070	0.048	0.0213	0.0489	0.0427	0.1640	0.0269	0.0235	0.0189	0.0165
0.068	0.027	0.0395	0.0865	0.0758	0.2118	0.0449	0.0393	0.0358	0.0314
0.093	0.047	0.0421	0.0918	0.0769	0.2162	0.0467	0.0392	0.0394	0.0330
0.077	0.059	0.0165	0.0446	0.0384	0.1533	0.0235	0.0203	0.0167	0.0144

(*continued*)

TABLE 4.5 (Continued)

Mean	Geom. Mean	Ln(1 + E) − Ln(1 + G)	Variance	Variance/ (1 + E)²	MAD	MAD²	MAD²/ (1 + E)²	Semivar.	Semivar./ (1 + E)²
0.091	0.070	0.0191	0.0513	0.0431	0.1716	0.0295	0.0247	0.0194	0.0163
0.058	0.038	0.0188	0.0483	0.0431	0.1663	0.0276	0.0247	0.0193	0.0173
0.087	0.067	0.0183	0.0485	0.0410	0.1644	0.0270	0.0229	0.0206	0.0175
0.065	0.047	0.0170	0.0379	0.0335	0.1435	0.0206	0.0182	0.0164	0.0145
0.076	0.059	0.0162	0.0401	0.0346	0.1454	0.0211	0.0182	0.0173	0.0149
0.089	0.071	0.0162	0.0408	0.0345	0.1655	0.0274	0.0231	0.0213	0.0180
Beta			0.4287	0.4972	0.1397	0.8048	0.9307	1.0595	1.2297
RMSQ%			0.17	0.18	0.70	0.40	0.42	0.35	0.35

TABLE 4.6 Variance, VaR, and CVaR Approximations to Geometric Mean for 16 Equity Markets During the Twentieth Century

Mean	Geom. Mean	Ln(1 + E) − Ln(1 + G)	Variance/ (1 + E)²	VaR	[(VaR + E)/ K]²	[(VaR + E)/ K]²/ (1 + E)²	CVaR	CVaR²	CVaR²/ (1 + E)²
0.092	0.077	0.0134	0.0268	0.2281	0.0375	0.0315	0.3022	0.0913	0.0766
0.053	0.030	0.0226	0.0486	0.2809	0.0410	0.0370	0.3325	0.1105	0.0996
0.073	0.060	0.0124	0.0249	0.2193	0.0314	0.0273	0.2572	0.0661	0.0574
0.067	0.050	0.0160	0.0352	0.2113	0.0284	0.0250	0.2504	0.0627	0.0551
0.060	0.036	0.0237	0.0489	0.2857	0.0440	0.0391	0.3441	0.1184	0.1053
0.085	0.035	0.0470	0.0908	0.3126	0.0580	0.0493	0.4666	0.2178	0.1850
0.070	0.048	0.0213	0.0427	0.2520	0.0381	0.0333	0.3394	0.1152	0.1005
0.068	0.027	0.0395	0.0758	0.3702	0.0705	0.0618	0.5008	0.2508	0.2199
0.093	0.047	0.0421	0.0769	0.4155	0.0948	0.0794	0.5652	0.3194	0.2676
0.077	0.059	0.0165	0.0384	0.2028	0.0288	0.0248	0.2773	0.0769	0.0663

(continued)

TABLE 4.6 (Continued)

Mean	Geom. Mean	Ln(1 + E) − Ln(1 + G)	Variance/ (1 + E)²	VaR	[(VaR + E)/ K]²	[(VaR + E)/ K]²/ (1 + E)²	CVaR	CVaR²	CVaR²/ (1 + E)²
0.091	0.070	0.0191	0.0431	0.1964	0.0303	0.0255	0.2917	0.0851	0.0715
0.058	0.038	0.0188	0.0431	0.2701	0.0395	0.0353	0.3344	0.1118	0.0999
0.087	0.067	0.0183	0.0410	0.2476	0.0412	0.0348	0.3250	0.1057	0.0894
0.065	0.047	0.0170	0.0335	0.2513	0.0367	0.0324	0.2992	0.0895	0.0790
0.076	0.059	0.0162	0.0346	0.2050	0.0291	0.0251	0.3251	0.1057	0.0912
0.089	0.071	0.0162	0.0345	0.3004	0.0556	0.0469	0.3441	0.1184	0.0999
		Beta	0.4972	0.0874	0.5066	0.5900	0.0675	0.1669	0.1947
		RMSQ%	0.18	0.68	0.61	0.60	0.55	0.49	0.46

Alternative Measures of Risk • 145

FIGURE 4.12 Ln(1 + E) − Ln(1 + G) versus Variance for 16 Equity Markets During the Twentieth Century.

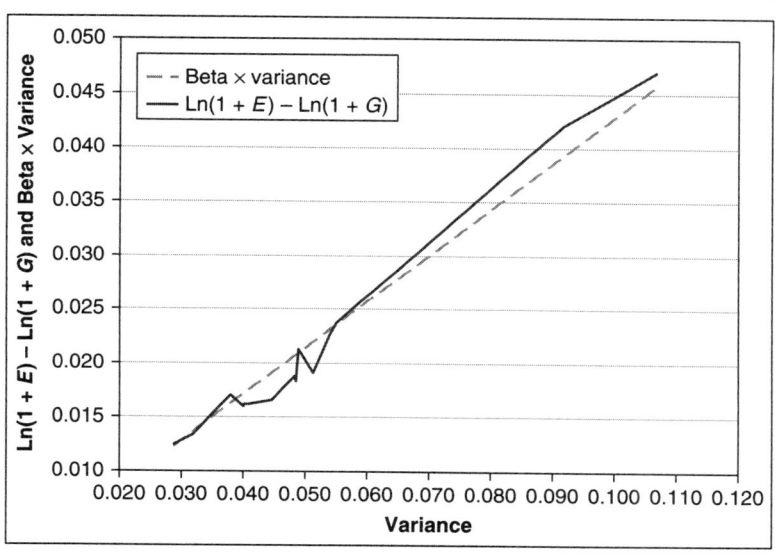

FIGURE 4.13 Ln(1 + E) − Ln(1 + G) versus MAD^2 for 16 Equity Markets During the Twentieth Century.

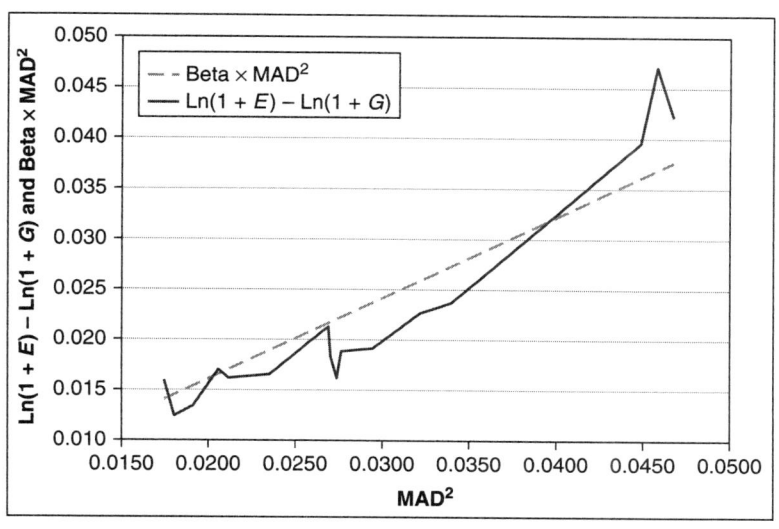

FIGURE 4.14 Ln(1 + E) − Ln(1 + G) versus Semivariance for 16 Equity Markets During the Twentieth Century.

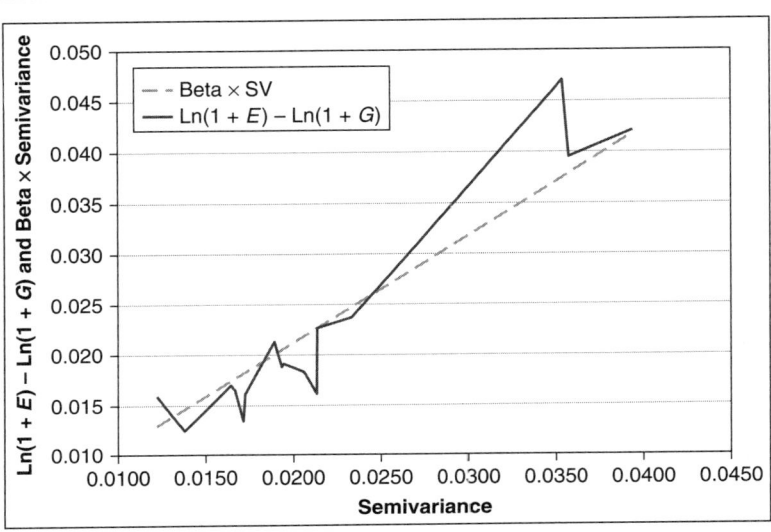

FIGURE 4.15 Ln(1 + E) − Ln(1 + G) versus $[(VaR + E/K)^2]/(1 + E)^2$ for 16 Equity Markets During the Twentieth Century.

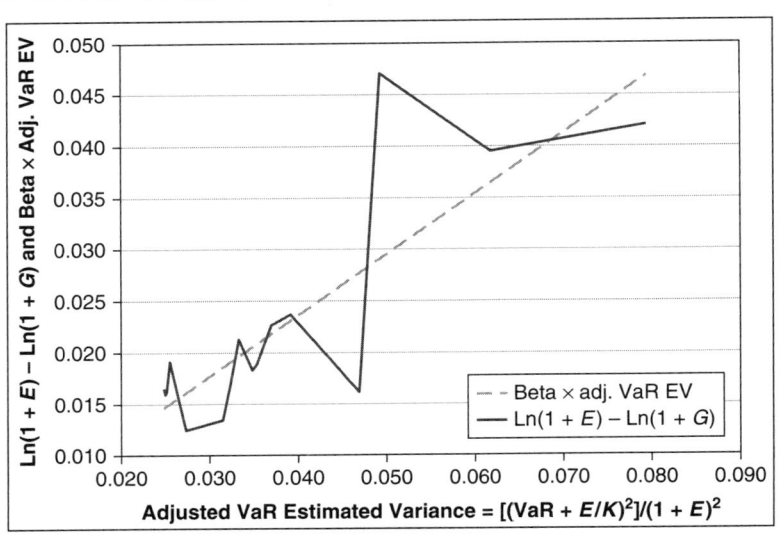

FIGURE 4.16 Ln(1 + E) − Ln(1 + G) versus CVaR^2/(1 + E)^2 for 16 Equity Markets During the Twentieth Century.

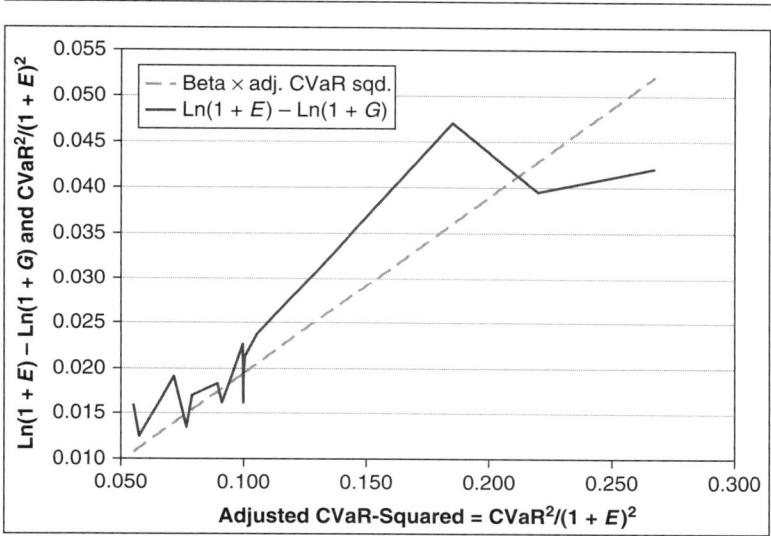

Remarkably, for the DMS database whose large losses are shown in Figure 4.11, VaR and CVaR—which are put forth as the measures to use in case of such large deviations—have substantially greater errors of approximation than do the functions of variance. More generally, in both databases, functions of variance gave the smallest root-mean-squared errors among all functions of the risk measures tried.

CAVEAT AND CONCLUSION

Conceivably, some other function of semivariance, MAD, VaR, or CVaR would perform better than those tried here. Conceivably, the ordering of root-mean-squares for the functions considered here would be quite different for a different database or a different approximated utility function. That remains to be seen. If such is to be shown, proponents of alternative risk measures need to get beyond their current line of argument, which goes roughly as follows: return distributions are not normal; therefore, mean variance is inapplicable; therefore, my risk measure is best.

5

THE LIKELIHOOD OF VARIOUS RETURN DISTRIBUTIONS

With Anthony Tessitore, Ansel Tessitore, and Nilufer Usmen[1]

INTRODUCTION

In prior chapters, it was argued that:

- The maximization of expected utility should be the standard for *rational* choice among probability distributions in single-period decision situations with known odds (Chapter 1).
- A careful choice from a mean-variance efficient frontier will approximately maximize expected utility for a wide range of concave (risk-averse) utility functions and real-world portfolio return distributions (Chapters 2 and 3).

- Variance is apparently at least as good as any other frequently proposed risk measure in approximately maximizing EU = $E \log(1 + \text{return})$ (Chapter 4).

We conclude from this that mean-variance analysis can benefit investors even when return distributions are not normally distributed. The flip side of this conclusion is that it may *not* be true that an efficient portfolio with expected return E and standard deviation σ will have, for example, approximately 95 percent of its return distribution within $E \pm 2\sigma$. Statements such as this must assume some form of probability distribution.

The authors of the present chapter explored probability distributions descriptive of—or that might be likely to have generated—the returns in the DMS database described in Chapter 3. The present chapter presents the results of this research. The chapter's primary objectives are to:

1. Show kinds of distributions that may well have generated past return series.
2. Illustrate a methodology that could be used in the future to estimate portfolio return distributions generally.

The study reported here includes methodology used by Markowitz and Usmen (1996a and b) and by Alparslan, Tessitore, and Usmen (2013). These papers analyze daily returns on the S&P 500. They assume that, when not all odds are known, the rational decision maker (RDM) will maximize expected utility (EU) using probability beliefs (PB) in place of unknown "objective" probabilities. A corollary of this EU/PB rule is that, as data accumulate, probability beliefs are updated according to Bayes' rule. This is the view of rational decision making under uncertainty adopted by Markowitz (1959), Chapter 12, based on the axiomatic approach of Savage (1954).

Bayes' rule requires prior beliefs in order to calculate posterior beliefs from data. On the other hand, the data themselves imply a certain statistic, the *Bayes factor*, that indicates how Bayesian decision makers would "shift" beliefs among various hypotheses.[2] Bayes factors help summarize the practical implications of a data set for Bayesian decision makers, whom Hildreth (1963) refers to as "remote clients," that is, Bayesians who are not known to the Bayesian statistician and who may hold differing prior beliefs.

Markowitz and Usmen (1996b) report Bayes factors implied by their data for a large class of probability distributions called the *Pearson family*. This family includes many well-known probability distributions, such as the normal, Student's *t*, gamma (chi-squared), Cauchy, beta (of the first and second kinds), uniform, and exponential distributions. Markowitz and Usmen find, for example, that Bayesians should shift their beliefs by a factor 10^{74} *against* the "best" of the normal return distributions *in favor of* a Student's *t* distribution with between 4 and 5 degrees of freedom. Alparslan et al. compute Bayes factors between the "winners" among Pearson distributions and the "winners" of a different family, namely, the stable Paretian whose distributions are sometimes hypothesized as generating returns (Mandelbrot 1963). Alparslan et al. (2013) find that the winners among the Pearson family trounce the winners among the stable Paretian family.

The following section of this chapter provides background on Bayes factors. This is followed by a section that serves two purposes: it introduces the Pearson family of distributions, and it summarizes the main results of the Markowitz and Usmen study. The latter study determined not only which Pearson distribution had the greatest likelihood of generating the observed data but also which had sufficiently favorable Bayes factors that a Bayesian remote client should shift probability beliefs very little against them, as compared to those against which the shift in belief should be massive.

These sections—on Bayes factors, Pearson distributions, and the main results of the Markowitz and Usmen study—will constitute just short of the first half of this chapter. The second half of the chapter considers the DMS database. It examines 20 return series, namely:

1. The real equity returns of the 16 countries originally tabulated by Dimson et al. (2002). (We met these already in Chapters 3 and 4.)
2. Three countries that Dimson et al. added subsequently
3. The combined real returns of all 19 countries

We call the latter return set the *Ensemble* and consider it to be a sample of returns from the distribution a Bayesian would have if he or she thought that the next return from a portfolio would be equally likely from a distribution like any of the 19 country distributions. It was beyond the scope of the project reported here to perform a similar analysis on each of the 19 countries individually. However, associated Pearson distributions, as well as moments and histograms, help characterize the remarkably diverse empirical distributions to which investors would in fact have been subject during the twentieth century.

BAYES FACTORS

We start by defining Bayes' rule when:

1. There are only a finite number (n) of hypotheses (H_i) that the RDM considers possible explanations of the data.
2. There are only a finite number of possible "observations" that could be generated by any of these hypotheses.

Let:

- $P(H_i)$ be the probability that an RDM assigns to the ith hypothesis before O (the data) is observed.
- $L(O|H_i)$ be the probability (a.k.a. the "likelihood") of observing O if hypothesis H_i were true.
- $P(H_i|O)$ be the probability that the RDM assigns hypothesis H_i given the observation.

Bayes' rule asserts that

$$P(H_i|O) = \frac{P(H_i) \cdot L(O|H_i)}{\sum_{j=1}^{n} P(H_j) \cdot L(O|H_j)} \qquad (1)$$

Equation (1) requires prior beliefs $P(H_i)$ in order to get posterior beliefs $P(H_i|O)$. On the other hand, the ratio (for example) of $P(H_1|O)$ to $P(H_2|O)$ is

$$\frac{P(H_1|O)}{P(H_2|O)} = \frac{L(O|H_1)}{L(O|H_2)} \cdot \frac{P(H_1)}{P(H_2)} \qquad (2a)$$

that is,

$$\frac{P(H_1|O)}{P(H_2|O)} = B_{12} \frac{P(H_1)}{P(H_2)} \qquad (2b)$$

where

$$B_{12} = \frac{L(O|H_1)}{L(O|H_2)} \qquad (2c)$$

B_{12} is called the Bayes factor between H_1 and H_2. It shows the direction and amount by which a Bayesian RDM would shift its prior belief ratio $P(H_1)/P(H_2)$ to its posterior belief ratio of $P(H_1|O)$ to $P(H_2|O)$ on the basis of observation O. Its computation does not require priors.

The observation O in Equations (1) and (2) may be a set of numbers such as the historical returns on a portfolio. If T items in a series are assumed to be independent draws from either the distribution specified by hypothesis H_1 or that specified by hypothesis H_2, then the Bayes factor between the two hypotheses is

$$B_{12} = \frac{\prod_{t=1}^{T} p_t}{\prod_{t=1}^{T} q_t} \qquad (3a)$$

or

$$\log(B_{12}) = \sum_{t=1}^{T} \log(p_t) - \sum_{t=1}^{T} \log(q_t) \qquad (3b)$$

where p_t and q_t are the probabilities of item t if, respectively, hypothesis H_1 or hypothesis H_2 is true. The expression on the right-hand side of Equation (3a) is referred to as the *likelihood ratio*, LH_p/LH_q; that in Equation (3b) is the *log-likelihood ratio* $LLH_p - LLH_q$. According to Equation (2), B_{12} shows the shift in belief ratios—between prior and posterior—implied by the data. We will use the common logarithm $\log_{10}$ in computing LLH; therefore, Equation (3b) shows the number of orders of magnitude of the shift specified by Equation (3a).

The probability distributions of the Pearson family are continuous rather than discrete, with each characterized by a probability-density function $f(x)$ rather than a finite number of probabilities. In this case, the Bayes factor between hypothesis H_1—that a series of items is generated by a distribution with density function $f(x)$—versus hypothesis H_2—that the density function is $g(x)$—is defined to be:

$$B_{12} = \frac{\prod_{t=1}^{T} f(x_t)}{\prod_{t=1}^{T} g(x_t)} \qquad (4a)$$

$$\log(B_{12}) = \sum_{t=1}^{T}\log[f(x_t)] - \sum_{t=1}^{T}\log[g(x)] \quad (4b)$$

where x_t is the *t*th item in the series. Since the distributions of H_1 and H_2 are continuous, there is zero probability of getting any specific set of returns, just as there is zero probability that a uniformly distributed random variable will be precisely 0.5. However, the probability that a number drawn with density $f(x)$ will fall in a small interval of length Δx is approximately $f(x)\Delta x$. Thus, if we define the observation O to be that of T random values falling in intervals of length Δx centered on $x_1, x_2, ..., x_T$, then B_{12} and its log are approximately

$$B_{12} = \frac{\prod_{t=1}^{T} f(x_t)\Delta x}{\prod_{t=1}^{T} g(x_t)\Delta x} \quad (5a)$$

$$\log(B_{12}) = \sum_{t=1}^{T}\log[f(x_t)] + T\Delta x - \left\{\sum_{t=1}^{T}\log[g(x_t)] + T\Delta x\right\}$$

$$= \sum_{t=1}^{T}\log[f(x_t)] - \sum_{t=1}^{T}\log[g(x_t)] \quad (5b)$$

Note that this approximation does not depend on the size of Δx.

TRANSFORMED VARIABLES

Markowitz and Usmen

1. Let $x_t = \log(\text{S\&P 500}_t/\text{S\&P 500}_{t-1})$.
2. Found the Pearson distribution that maximized LH with x_t thus defined.

3. Computed the Bayes factors between this distribution and various alternative distributions.

In particular, the Bayes factor of 74 orders of magnitude against the normal with greatest LH in favor of a Student's t with between 4 and 5 degrees of freedom, cited earlier, was computed this way. In the present chapter, we will consider alternative definitions of x as well as alternative Pearson distributions. Specifically, we will compute LH and LLH for various Pearson distributions with x defined alternatively as $(1 + R)$, $\log(1 + R)$, and $(1 + R)^\alpha$ for various α. The reason for these alternative choices for the argument x in density functions $f(x)$ will be discussed later. Here we note a technical point concerning how densities *must* be transformed when x is thus redefined.

A density function $f(x)$ is the derivative of a cumulative probability function $F(x)$:

$$f(x) = \frac{dF(x)}{dx} \tag{6}$$

where $F(x)$ is the probability that a random draw will not exceed x. If we change to a new variable y such that

$$x = h(y) \tag{7a}$$

with a positive first derivative everywhere,

$$\frac{dx}{dy} = h'(y) \tag{7b}$$
$$> 0$$

then

$$G(y_0) = F[h(y_0)] \tag{8}$$

is the probability that a randomly drawn value of y will be less than some specified value y_0. In other words, to calculate

$$G(y_0) = \text{Prob}(y \le y_0) \tag{9}$$

use Equation (7a) to determine the corresponding x_0 and set $G(y_0) = F(x_0)$. But it is *not* true that the density of the new variable is $g[h(y)]$. Rather,

$$\begin{aligned} g(y) &= \frac{dG(y)}{dy} \\ &= \frac{dF[h(y)]}{dy} \\ &= \frac{dF}{dx} \cdot \frac{dx}{dy} \\ &= f[h(y)] \cdot h'(y) \end{aligned} \tag{10}$$

A hypothesis about the probability distribution of y is also a hypothesis about the probability distribution of x. For example, if

$$y = \log(x)$$

then the hypothesis that y is normally distributed (with mean m and standard deviation σ) is the same as the hypothesis that

x is lognormally distributed. The density functions for y and x are, respectively,

$$g(y) = \frac{1}{\sqrt{2\pi}\sigma} e^{-(y-m)^2/2\sigma^2} \tag{11a}$$

$$f(x) = \frac{1}{\sqrt{2\pi}x\sigma} e^{-[\log(x)-m]^2/2\sigma^2} \tag{11b}$$

Because of the x^{-1} factor in Equation (11b), one would get a different LLH from summing $\log[f(x)]$ than from summing $\log[g(x)]$. Which is correct? The answer is that either is correct as long as the same variable is used for all hypotheses. For example, Markowitz and Usmen consider only probability distributions of $\log(1 + R)$; therefore, it is permissible for them to consider only alternative probability distributions of this variable. In contrast, the present chapter considers Pearson distributions of $(1 + R)$, $\log(1 + R)$, and $(1 + R)^\alpha$ for various α. It would be like comparing apples and oranges—or, more aptly in this case, like comparing dollars, pounds, and euros—if we compared the sums of the log densities of $(1 + R)$, $\log(1 + R)$, and $(1 + R)^{1/2}$. We have to translate all results to a common currency. We chose to translate all densities back to $x = (1 + R)$.

COMPOUND HYPOTHESES

Thus far we have discussed the Bayes factor for the shift in belief ratios among *simple hypotheses* as opposed to *compound hypotheses*. A simple hypothesis asserts that an observation was generated by a specific probability distribution such as a normal distribution $N(m_0\ \sigma_0)$ with a specific mean and standard deviation m_0 and σ_0. A compound hypothesis asserts that the observation was generated by some distribution within a class of distributions. For example, hypothesis H_N might assert that x is generated by *some* normal distribution, as compared to H_S, which asserts that it is generated by *some* Student's t distribution.

The computation of a Bayes factor between compound hypotheses, such as $B(H_N, H_S)$, raises issues that are not encountered in computing Bayes factors between simple hypotheses. Specifically, it requires some kind of assumption about how prior beliefs are distributed *within* the hypothesized class of distributions; for example, $B(H_N, H_S)$ depends on how the total prior probability assigned to $P(H_N)$ is spread among specific hypotheses within this class. Akaike (1974, 1977, 1979), Schwarz (1978), and Alparslan et al. have proposals for evaluating the Bayes factor between compound hypotheses.[3] As we shall review toward the end of the next section, Markowitz and Usmen show that even if one makes certain assumptions about priors that are *highly favorable to* H_N, as compared to a class H_K (of "Type IV distributions" with high kurtosis), *nevertheless* the implied Bayes factor $B(H_N, H_K)$ indicates a massive shift against H_N in favor of H_K.

We will not explore here the relative merits of these approaches to computing Bayes factors among compound hypotheses. In the empirical sections of the present chapter, we will primarily confine ourselves to questions for which Bayes factors between simple hypotheses provide answers.

THE PEARSON FAMILY

Markowitz and Usmen report Bayes factors among Pearson distributions for x equal to the daily log returns of the S&P 500, that is, equal to $\log(S\&P_t/S\&P_{t-1})$. They divide their sample into four subsamples including:

S1 (weekdays): returns from one day's close to the following day's close

S2 (normal weekends): returns from Friday's close to Monday's close

and two other categories.

We illustrate certain features of Pearson distributions in terms of their largest subsample, S1.

The Pearson family consists of probability distributions whose probability densities $f(x)$ satisfy the following differential equation:

$$\frac{df}{dx} = \frac{(x-a)f(x)}{b_0 + b_1 x + b_2 x^2} \qquad (12)$$

K. Pearson classified the solutions to Equation (12) into various "types." Some of these are named distributions or have named distributions as special cases; some are not. For example, the Type IV distribution is not a standard, named distribution, but its symmetric special case, denoted by Pearson as Type VII, is more commonly known as the Student's *t* distribution. The Cauchy distribution, in turn, is a special case of the Student's *t* distribution. Stuart and Ord (1994), Chapter 6, contains an extensive discussion of Equation (12) and its solution. Further information about specific types may be found in Stuart and Ord's index under Type I, Type II, and so on.

The classification of solutions of Equation (12) into types is facilitated by substituting

$$X = x - a$$

and rewriting the equation in terms of log *f*, obtaining

$$\frac{d \log f}{dX} = \frac{X}{B_0 + B_1 X + B_2 X^2} \tag{13}$$

where

$$B_0 = b_0 + a^2(1 + b_2)$$
$$B_1 = a(1 + 2b_2)$$
$$B_2 = b_2$$

The general nature of the solution depends on:

1. Whether or not $B_2 = b_2 = 0$.
2. If $B_2 \neq 0$, whether the quadratic in the denominator of the right-hand side of Equation (13) has real or complex roots. If its roots are real, the solution further depends on whether (a) the roots are of the same sign or (b) the roots are of opposite signs.

If the roots of the quadratic are complex, then the density function that solves Equations (12) and (13) extends infinitely in both directions. This is consistent with the fact that the denominator of Equation (13) is never zero for any real X. If the roots of the denominator of Equation (13) are real and of the same sign, then $f(x) = 0$ beyond some bound in one direction. If the roots are real and of opposite sign, then $f(x) = 0$ beyond both an upper and a lower limit.

In the case of the S1 subsample, all Pearson distributions H with a Bayes factor $B(\hat{H}, H)$ less than 10^{10}—where $\hat{H}$ is the LH-maximizing Pearson distribution—were of Type IV, including its Type VII symmetric special case. Type IV distributions are associated with complex roots, and therefore have density functions that extend infinitely in both directions. Let

$$M_3 = E(R - ER)^3/\sigma^3 \qquad (14a)$$
$$M_4 = E(R - ER)^4/\sigma^4 \qquad (14b)$$

M_3 is a measure of the skewness of a distribution, and M_4 is a measure of its kurtosis ("fat-tailedness"). For the normal distribution, $M_3 = 0$ and $M_4 = 3$. Table 5.1 here has the same content as Table 3a in Markowitz and Usmen (1996b). It shows (for the S1 subsample) the means, standard deviations, and M_3 values that maximize LH for Type IV distributions with M_4 set at different levels. It also shows LLH, max LLH − LLH, and the Bayes factor

$$B(\hat{H}, H) = \max \text{LH}/\text{LH}$$

TABLE 5.1 Likelihood-Maximizing Parameter Combinations for Various Values of M_4, Weekdays (S_1)

M_4	Mean × 1,000	Std. Dev × 1,000	M_3	LLH	Max LLH − LLH	Max LH/ LH
3	0.545	7.68	0.000*	−29.839	74.254	>10^{74}
Sample	0.515	7.51	0.068	41.227	3.188	1,542.00
12	0.500	7.79	0.038	44.415	0.000	1.00
18	0.500	7.91	0.034	44.413	0.002	1.01
1,000	0.510	8.06	0.022	43.859	0.556	3.60
100,000	0.500	8.06	0.022	43.844	0.571	3.72

*Normal case; therefore $M_3 = 0$.
Source: Markowitz and Usmen (1996b), Table 3.

for these distributions. The one exception is that the first row of the table shows this information for the normal distribution, and therefore reflects only distributions with $M_3 = 0$ as well as $M_4 = 3$. We see, for example, that the LH-maximizing value of M_4 (about $M_4 = 12$) is not equal to the sample value of M_4 for S1 (listed elsewhere in Markowitz and Usmen as $M_4 = 5.69$). In fact, the Bayes factor between $\hat{H}$ with $M_4 = 12$ and the LH-maximizing Pearson distribution with $M_4 = 5.69$ is more than 1,500. On the other hand, the Bayes factor between $\hat{H}$ and the LH-maximizing Pearson distribution with $M_4 = 100,000$ is only 3.72.

Table 5.2 here, based on Table 6a of Markowitz and Usmen (1996b), shows LLH, max LLH − LLH, and the Bayes

TABLE 5.2 Likelihood as a Function of M_3 with Values of Mean, Standard Deviation, and M_4 Set at Their Likelihood-Maximizing Value in Table 5.1, Weekdays (S_1)

M_3	LLH	Max LLH − LLH	Max LH/LH
−0.740	32.902	11.513	3.3×10^{11}
−0.555	38.227	6.188	1.5×10^{6}
−0.370	41.639	2.776	597.00
−0.185	43.612	0.803	6.35
0.0000	44.391	0.024	1.06
0.038*	44.415	0.000	1.00
0.185	44.066	0.349	2.23
0.370†	42.605	1.810	65.00
0.555	39.841	4.574	37,497.00
0.740	35.405	9.010	1.0×10^{9}

*LH-maximizing value of M_3.
†Sample M_3.
Source: Markowitz and Usmen (1996b), Table 6.

factor max LH/LH for distributions with mean, standard deviation, and M_4 fixed at their LH-maximizing values in our Table 5.1, but with varying M_3. In particular, it shows that the Bayes factor between $\hat{H}$ and the symmetric case with $M_3 = 0.0$ is 1.06. Thus there is only a 6 percent shift in belief ratio called for between the LH-maximizing Type IV distribution and a symmetric (Student's t) case.

The Student's t distribution is widely used to test the significance of the mean of a sample from a normal distribution when the standard deviation of the distribution is not known but must be estimated from the sample itself with D_f degrees of freedom. In this statistical application, D_f is an integer, but the distribution is defined for noninteger D_f. The relationship between M_4 and D_f is

$$M_4 = 3 + 6/(D_f - 4), \qquad \text{for } D_f > 4 \qquad (15)$$

as $D_f \to \infty$, $M_4 \to 3$, and the Student's t approaches the normal distribution. For $D_f \leq 4$, M_4 is infinite.

Table 5.3 here [extracted from Table 7 of Markowitz and Usmen (1996b)] shows LLH for Student's t distributions with various degrees of freedom and the corresponding M_4. The means and standard deviations used here are those that maximize LH among Student's t distributions with the specified degrees of freedom. We see that the (approximately) best Student's t distribution has $D_f = 4.5$; therefore, $M_4 = 15$. Its LLH of 44.402 is just slightly less than the grand maximum of 44.415 among all Pearson distributions. The Student's t distribution with $D_f = 4$, and therefore with an infinite M_4, has an LLH of 43.669. Thus the Bayes factor between the LH-maximizing Student's t and the LH-maximizing Type IV distribution with infinite M_4 is less than an order of magnitude. This is as compared to the normal distribution, which has a Bayes factor of $44.4 - (-29.8) = 74.2$ orders of magnitude.

The comparisons described in these tables are among simple hypotheses, such as the LH-maximizing Student's t distribution versus the LH-maximizing normal distribution.

TABLE 5.3 Degrees of Freedom, M_4, and LLH of Student's t Distributions for the Markowitz and Usmen Data, Weekdays (S_1)

DF	M_4	LLH
1.50	Infinite	−38.205
2.00	Infinite	5.382
2.50	Infinite	26.169
3.00	Infinite	36.518
4.00	Infinite	43.669
4.00006	100,000	43.811
4.006	1,000	43.822
4.01	603	43.833
4.10	63	44.015
4.30	23	44.200
4.50	15	44.402
5.00	9	44.027
6.00	6	41.827
7.00	5	38.831
10.00	4	29.576
Infinite	3	−29.839

Source: Markowitz and Usmen (1996b), Table 7.

Markowitz and Usmen also consider compound hypotheses such as H_N that $\log(1 + R)$ was generated by *some* normal distribution versus H_K that it was generated by *some* Type IV distribution with $M_4 \geq 12$. Markowitz and Usmen make certain plausible (we think) assumptions about priors—for example, that the Bayesian assigns at least some small prior probability to M_4 being in the range [12, 100,000] (their calculation assumes that this probability is *at least* 0.01)—and conclude that the Bayes factor $B(H_K, H_N)$ is *at least* 10^{64} against the normal, in favor of some Type IV with $M_4 \in$ [12, 100,000].

If $D_f \leq 2.0$, the Student's *t* distribution has infinite variance, in which case mean-variance analysis is meaningless. Table 5.3 shows that, for subsample S_1, there is a Bayes factor of about 10^{39} against $M_4 = 2$ in favor of $M_4 = 4.5$. An analysis (similar to that between the compound hypotheses H_N and H_K described earlier) can be constructed to show that the Bayesian should shift massively *against* the compound hypothesis that the S&P 500 log return is *some* Pearson distribution with infinite variance.

The stable Paretian family, an alternative to the Pearson family of distributions, includes only (1) normal distributions and (2) distributions with infinite variance. Thus, if one assumes that a return distribution is stable Paretian and one rejects normality, then one must conclude that the distribution has an infinite variance. Alparslan et al. find that Bayesians should shift belief massively against the compound hypothesis that $y = \log(\text{S\&P 500}_t/\text{S\&P 500}_{t-1})$ is generated by *some* stable Paretian distribution in favor of the hypothesis that it was generated by some Student's *t* distribution or other Pearson Type IV distribution. This, combined with the Markowitz and Usmen results reported earlier, implies that the Bayesian should shift belief massively against the compound hypothesis that y was generated by a distribution with infinite variance, assuming that the return distribution is either a Pearson or a stable Paretian distribution.

We saw in Chapters 3 and 4 that mean-variance approximations have no problem approximating EU = $E \log(1 + R)$ for *annual* returns of asset classes such as large-cap stocks. As reviewed in Chapter 2, Levy and Markowitz (1979) confirmed that mean-variance approximations become more accurate as Δt shrinks. Therefore, mean-variance approximations should have no problem approximating EU for long positions in the S&P 500 held for a day, for typical concave $U(R)$. But if a complex, highly leveraged investment strategy is based on the assumption that S&P 500 returns are lognormal, the result may be disastrous, as many have found.

THE DMS DATABASE

Tables 5.4a and 5.4b list 19 countries, of which 16 are the countries for which Dimson et al. originally reported returns during the twentieth century, 1900–2000. The other 3 were added in subsequent editions of Dimson et al., as were returns for more recent years. While we have added the three countries to the list analyzed in this chapter, we continue to include only real returns from 1900 through 2000 for comparability with Chapters 3 and 4.

Table 5.4a shows the arithmetic mean, standard deviation, M_3, and M_4 for each of the 19 countries and for the Ensemble of all annual real returns. We view the latter as a sample from the

TABLE 5.4a Sample Moments and Pearson Types for $X = (1 + R)$

		Arith. Mean	Std. Dev.	M_3	M_4	Pearson Type IV	Pearson Type I	Pearson Type VI
1	Australia	1.092	0.18	−0.24	2.97		x	
2	Belgium	1.053	0.23	0.97	5.68	x		
3	Canada	1.073	0.17	0.11	2.87		x	
4	Denmark	1.067	0.20	1.98	10.26			x
5	Finland	1.101	0.30	1.40	8.13	x		
6	France	1.061	0.23	0.44	2.70		x	
7	Germany	1.085	0.33	1.51	8.47	x		
8	Ireland	1.070	0.22	0.66	3.79			x
9	Italy	1.068	0.29	0.75	5.23	x		
10	Japan	1.093	0.30	0.49	5.25	x		
11	Netherlands	1.077	0.21	1.15	6.19	x		
12	New Zealand	1.077	0.20	1.33	9.69	x		
13	Norway	1.065	0.26	2.58	15.87			x
14	South Africa	1.091	0.23	1.00	5.60	x		
15	Spain	1.058	0.22	0.84	5.14	x		
16	Sweden	1.087	0.22	0.60	4.27	x		
17	Switzerland	1.065	0.19	0.47	3.46	x		
18	United Kingdom	1.077	0.20	0.68	6.57	x		
19	United States	1.089	0.20	−0.17	2.64		x	
20	Ensemble	1.076	0.24	1.09	7.95	x		

Source: Dimson, Marsh, and Stauton database supplied by Morningstar.

TABLE 5.4b Sample Moments and Pearson Types for $X = \log(1 + R)$

		Arith. Mean	Std. Dev.	M_3	M_4	Pearson Type IV	Pearson Type I	Pearson Type VI
1	Australia	0.073	0.17	−0.75	3.64		x	
2	Belgium	0.029	0.21	0.10	3.32	x		
3	Canada	0.058	0.16	−0.33	2.93		x	
4	Denmark	0.050	0.17	0.85	5.68	x		
5	Finland	0.061	0.27	−0.19	4.91	x		
6	France	0.035	0.22	−0.08	2.63		x	
7	Germany	0.033	0.35	−2.96	24.47			x
8	Ireland	0.047	0.21	−0.24	4.65	x		
9	Italy	0.026	0.29	−0.96	6.81	x		
10	Japan	0.043	0.33	−2.29	14.74			x
11	Netherlands	0.056	0.19	0.27	3.91	x		
12	New Zealand	0.058	0.18	−0.55	8.66	x		
13	Norway	0.038	0.22	0.46	6.97	x		
14	South Africa	0.067	0.20	−0.10	5.11	x		
15	Spain	0.036	0.20	−0.02	3.68	x		
16	Sweden	0.063	0.20	−0.22	3.75	x		
17	Switzerland	0.046	0.18	−0.14	3.30	x		
18	United Kingdom	0.056	0.19	−0.80	7.52	x		
19	United States	0.067	0.20	−0.65	3.17		x	
20	Ensemble	0.050	0.22	−1.20	14.92	x		

Source: Dimson, Marsh, and Stauton database supplied by Morningstar.

belief distribution of a Bayesian who believes that next year's real return on some portfolio is equally likely to be drawn from one or another distribution like those of the 19 countries.

All but two countries had $M_3 > 0$; that is, most county real-return distributions were positively skewed, as was that of the Ensemble. The exceptional cases, with negative M_3, were Australia and the United States. All but three countries had $M_4 > 3$. In this case, the exceptions were Australia, Canada, and the United States.

The type of a Pearson distribution is determined by its M_3 and M_4 when these are finite. The last three columns of Table 5.4a indicate the type of the Pearson distribution with the same M_3 and M_4 as those of each of the 20 samples. We will refer to these as the "sample types" of the sample distributions. The table shows that 12 countries and the Ensemble had sample types of Type IV, and 4 (including the United States) had sample types of Type I. The remaining 3 had sample types of Type VI.

The numbered points in Figure 5.1 show the M_3 and M_4 of the 19 countries and the Ensemble. The figure also shows the Pearson types of certain regions of the (M_3, M_4) plane. The formula for the probability density function changes as one passes from one region to another; however, for fixed mean, standard deviation, and the x argument, $f(x)$ is a continuous function of (finite) M_3 and M_4. Thus, if two distributions straddle a boundary line, their distributions—both their $f(x)$ and their $F(x)$—will be close even though their names and formulas are different.

FIGURE 5.1 Sample (1 + R) and Pearson Boundaries.

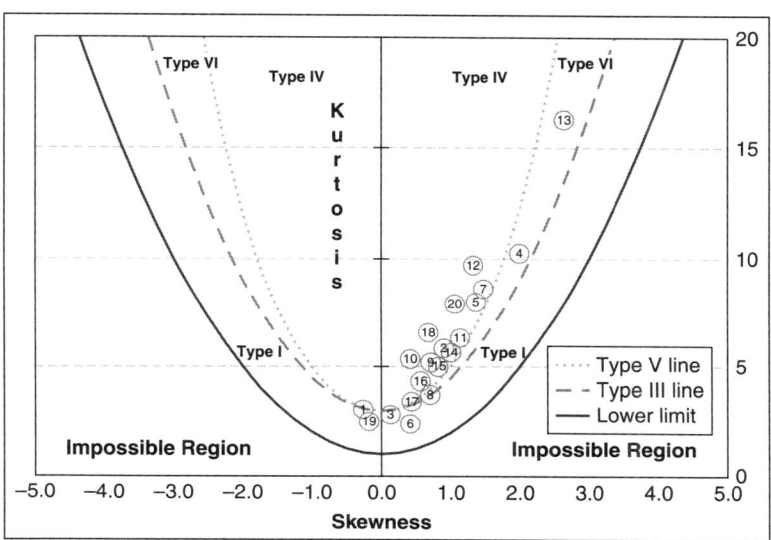

A Type I distribution is the solution to Equations (12) and (13) when the denominator of Equation (13) has real roots of opposite sign. It is also called a "beta distribution of the first kind." Its density function is zero beyond an upper and lower bound. A Type II distribution is a symmetric Type I. The Type VI distribution is the solution to Equations (12) and (13) when the denominator of Equation (13) has unequal real roots of the same sign. A Type V distribution has equal real roots. It is the curve in Figure 5.1 that separates the Type IV and Type VI regions. If $B_2 = 0$ in Equation (13), then the solution is a Type III, a.k.a. a gamma, distribution. It separates the Type I and Type VI regions.

The normal distribution has $M_3 = 0$ and $M_4 = 3$. Figure 5.1 shows that 1 (Australia), 3 (Canada), and 19 (the United States) had sample distributions with (M_3, M_4) near $(0, 3)$. The sample types of Australia, Canada, and the United States were of Type I, whose Pearson distributions have $f(y) = 0$ beyond an upper and a lower level. Nevertheless, perhaps these distributions have frequently considered probability levels—for example, Y such that $\text{Prob}(y \leq Y) = 0.01$—close to that of a normal distribution. We will refer to this as being "practically normal." In the next section, we consider how close its (M_3, M_4) needs to be to $(0, 3)$ for a distribution to be "practically normal."

Table 5.4b shows the sample arithmetic mean, standard deviation, M_3, and M_4 for $\log(1 + R)$ for the 19 countries and the Ensemble. In this case, all but four countries have negative M_3, as does the Ensemble. We see in Figure 5.2 that several countries had $\log(1 + R)$ samples with (M_3, M_4) near $(0, 3)$ and therefore had $(1 + R)$ distributions that were perhaps practically lognormal. A substantial exception is the Ensemble, which has an M_4 of almost 15. Its larger M_4, as compared to most of the other distributions, is because the Ensemble is a mixture of distributions. If y were a random variable drawn from some probability distribution that itself was drawn at random from some generating distribution, then y's mean, standard deviation, M_3, and M_4 would be functions of moments such as $E(V_H)$ and $V(E_H)$, where the first of these is the average, over all generated distributions, of the variances of the generated distribution, and the second is the

FIGURE 5.2 Sample Log (1 + R) and Pearson Boundaries.

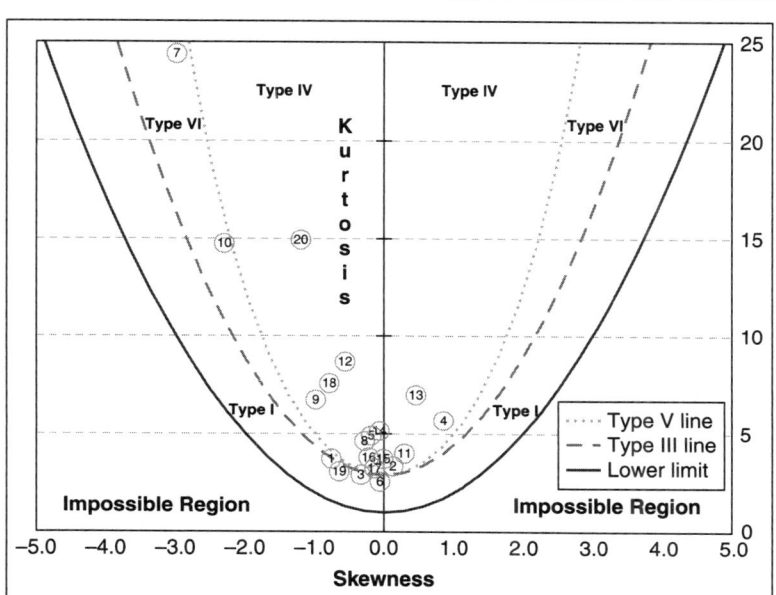

variance of the generated expected values.[4] In the special case wherein the generated distributions are normal—with fixed variance and mean distributed as a Type V distribution—then y would have a Student's t distribution. Its moments would, of course, conform to the general formulas given in Note 4.

PRACTICALLY NORMAL DISTRIBUTIONS

Table 5.4a shows that twentieth-century real equity returns for the United States had $M_3 = -0.167$ and $M_4 = 2.642$. Suppose—hypothetically—that U.S. real equity returns in the future will be drawn from a Pearson distribution with this M_3 and M_4. Would it be approximately correct that 2½ percent of the distribution would be below the mean minus about two standard deviations? More generally, is the cumulative probability distribution of this Pearson distribution close to that of a normal distribution for frequently considered probability levels? Similarly, Figure 5.2, based on Table 5.4b, shows that several country return distributions had $y = \log(1 + R)$ with (M_3, M_4) near $(0, 3)$. Are these (M_3, M_4) close enough to $(0, 3)$ that y may be considered normally distributed, and therefore $(1 + R)$ lognormally distributed, for "practical purposes"?

Tables 5.5a and 5.5b address this question for the lower 1 and 2.5 percent levels of Pearson distributions with various M_3 and M_4 combinations. Specifically, Tables 5.5a and 5.5b show, respectively, the Z level such that

$$\text{Prob}(z \leq -Z) = 0.01$$

and

$$\text{Prob}(z \leq -Z) = 0.025$$

for $z = (y - Ey)/\sigma$.

For example, in Table 5.5b, the entry for $M_3 = 0, M_4 = 3.0$ reminds us that the lower 2.5 percent level for the normal distribution is 1.96 rather than 2.0 exactly. The subscripts following the entries indicate Pearson type numbers or "N" for

TABLE 5.5a Lower 1 Percent Levels

M_4	−1.0	−0.5	−0.3	−0.2	−0.1	0.0	0.1	0.2	0.3	0.5	1.0
2.6		2.50$_I$	2.41$_I$	2.35	2.28	2.21$_{II}$	2.12	2.02	1.90$_I$	1.62$_I$	
3.0	2.68$_I$	2.62$_I$	2.52$_I$	2.46	2.39	2.33$_N$	2.25	2.16	2.06$_I$	1.82$_I$	1.00$_I$
4.0	2.99$_I$	2.74$_{IV}$	2.64$_{IV}$	2.59	2.53	2.47$_{VII}$	2.41	2.34	2.27$_{IV}$	2.10$_{IV}$	1.42$_I$
5.0	3.03$_{IV}$	2.78$_{IV}$	2.68$_{IV}$	2.63	2.58	2.53$_{VII}$	2.48	2.43	2.37$_{IV}$	2.23$_{IV}$	1.72$_{IV}$

TABLE 5.5b Lower 2.5 Percent Levels

M_4	−1.0	−0.5	−0.3	−0.2	−0.1	0.0	0.1	0.2	0.3	0.5	1.0
2.6		2.16$_I$	2.07$_I$	2.02	1.97	1.92$_{II}$	1.86	1.8	1.72$_I$	1.53$_I$	
3	2.41$_I$	2.18$_I$	2.09$_I$	2.05	2.01	1.96$_N$	1.91	1.86	1.79$_I$	1.65$_I$	1.00$_I$
4	2.42$_I$	2.18$_{IV}$	2.10$_{IV}$	2.06	2.03	1.99$_{VII}$	1.96	1.92	1.88$_{IV}$	1.78$_{IV}$	1.35$_I$
5	2.36$_{IV}$	2.15$_{IV}$	2.09$_{IV}$	2.06	2.03	2.00$_{VII}$	1.97	1.94	1.90$_{IV}$	1.83$_{IV}$	1.53$_{IV}$

normal. The general message of Table 5.5 is that—for variations of the size exhibited by the points in Figures 5.1 and 5.2 that we characterize as being near (0, 3)—deviations from zero by M_3 have a much greater effect on levels than do deviations from 3 by M_4. This is especially true of the 2.5 percent level, but it is also true of the 1 percent level. For example, in the $M_3 = 0$ column of Table 5.5b, the 2.5 percent level goes from 1.92 to 2.00 (an increase of 0.08) as M_4 goes from 2.6 to 5.0, whereas in the $M_4 = 3.0$ row of that table, the 2.5 percent level goes from 2.41 to 1.00 (a decrease of 1.41) as M_3 goes from -1 to $+1$. In Table 5.5a, the $M_3 = 0$ column shows that the 1 percent level goes from 2.21 to 2.53 as M_4 goes from 2.6 to 5.0, a difference of 0.32, whereas the $M_4 = 3$ row shows that the 1 percent level goes from 2.68 to 1.00 (the latter the same as for the 2.5 percent level when rounded to two places), a difference of -1.68.

If we fix M_3 at -0.3, -0.5, or -1.0 in Table 5.5b, we find that the 2.5 percent level is not an increasing function of M_4. Rather, it first increases and then decreases as M_4 increases. This seemed suspicious to us, but our own calculations reproduced the $M_4 = -0.3$ column of Johnson et al (1963). Thus, indeed, in these cases some of the "fat tail" that moves the 1 percent level to the left as M_4 increases is "borrowed" from the region between 1 and 2.5 percent. This reinforces the previous conclusion that the 2.5 percent level is especially more dependent on M_3 than on M_4.

Interpolating linearly between points in Tables 5.5a and 5.5b, we find that the 1 and 2.5 percent levels of the

Pearson distributions with the same M_3 and M_4 as the three "near normal" sample distributions are approximately

Country	M_3	M_4	1% Level	2.5% Level
Australia	−0.24	2.97	2.48	2.06
Canada	0.11	2.87	2.20	1.89
United States	−0.17	2.64	2.29	1.98

This is as compared to 2.33 and 1.96 for the normal distribution. Thus, to answer the question posed in the first paragraph of this section, a Pearson distribution with the same M_3 and M_4 as the United States had during the twentieth century has 1 and 2.5 percent levels quite close to those of the normal distribution. As to whether this will continue to be true for the next 101 years, starting now, whenever now is for the reader, is a matter for reflection and debate.

ILLUSTRATIVE HISTOGRAMS

Figure 5.3 shows the historical return frequencies of the United States (Type I), Norway (Type VI), and three Type IV samples, namely, the United Kingdom, Germany, and the Ensemble. These histograms help us to "see behind" the summary numbers presented in Tables 5.4a and 5.4b. In particular, out of 101 years, Germany had seven real returns greater than 50 percent, with three being close to or exceeding 100 percent. On the other hand, it had only one loss that exceeded 50 percent, but this was its roughly 90 percent loss following

FIGURE 5.3 Sample Frequencies of Return for Four Countries and the Ensemble.

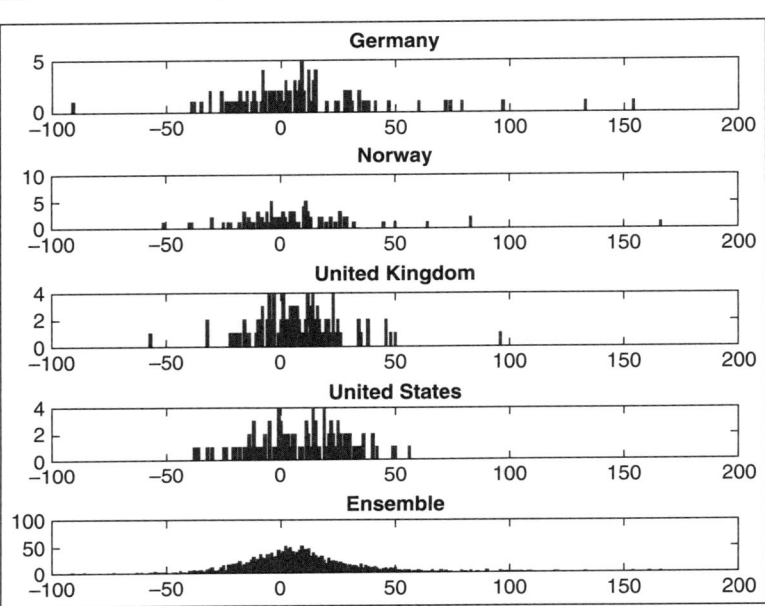

World War II. Because of the preponderance of large gains, its return sample (and therefore its $1 + R$ sample) was skewed to the right, with $M_3 = 1.51$. But when one takes logarithms, its 90 percent loss dominates its several large gains, resulting in $M_3 = -2.96$ for its $\log(1 + R)$ sample. Both its return distribution and its $\log(1 + R)$ sample had large M_4. Figure 5.1 shows that its return sample had the fourth-highest M_4, whereas Figure 5.2 shows that its $\log(1 + R)$ had by far the highest M_4. Germany's sample type was Type IV for $(1 + R)$ and Type VI for $\log(1 + R)$, but in both cases it was close to the Type V line.

Figure 5.3 shows that Norway had a few returns with gains close to or above 50 percent and one with a gain above

150 percent, whereas it had only one loss year around the −50 percent mark and none below that. Consequently, its log(1 + R), as well as its (1 + R), was skewed to the right. Specifically, Norway's log(1 + R) had an M_3 of 0.46. Figure 5.1 shows that its (1 + R) distribution had by far the largest M_3 and M_4, and its sample type was a solid Type VI. Figure 5.2 shows that the M_3 of its log(1 + R) sample, while positive, was less than that of Denmark (country 4), and its sample type is Type IV.

Figure 5.3 shows that the United Kingdom had four gains of nearly 50 percent, one gain of almost 100 percent, and one loss greater than 50 percent. Figures 5.1 and 5.2 show that, consequently, its (1 + R) was moderately skewed to the right, its log(1 + R) was moderately skewed to the left, and both had high, but far from highest, M_4. Both its (1 + R) and its log(1 + R) had sample types solidly within the Type IV region.

Figure 5.3 shows that the United States had a much more compact real return distribution than did Germany, Norway, or the United Kingdom. Its largest gain was a bit over 50 percent, and its largest loss was well short of 50 percent. Its (1 + R) distribution was slightly skewed to the left ($M_3 = -0.17$), and therefore its log(1 + R) was more substantially skewed to the left ($M_3 = -0.65$), but not as much as that of Germany ($M_3 = -2.96$), Japan ($M_3 = -2.29$), and Italy ($M_3 = -0.96$). The M_4 of its (1 + R) distribution was less than 3, and that of its log(1 + R) was slightly more than 3. Figures 5.1 and 5.2 show that both its (1 + R) and its log(1 + R) distributions had sample types in the Type I region, with (1 + R) near normal and log(1 + R) near the Type III line separating the Type I and Type IV regions.

The vertical axis for the histogram for the Ensemble had to be rescaled more radically than those of the others in Figure 5.3 because of the large number of observations portrayed. It is therefore hard to see some of its outliers, but all the outliers of the 19 country distributions are in the Ensemble sample, with smaller relative frequencies because the Ensemble has almost two thousand observations rather than 101. It nets out that its $(1 + R)$ sample was skewed to the right ($M_3 = 1.09$) and its $\log(1 + R)$ sample was skewed to the left ($M_3 = -1.20$), as were the majority of the individual country samples. The M_4 of both its $(1 + R)$ and its $\log(1 + R)$ samples were among the largest—$M_4 = 7.95$ for the former and $M_4 = 14.92$ for the latter—as is to be expected from a composite distribution.

NEAR LH-MAXIMIZING DISTRIBUTIONS FOR THE ENSEMBLE

In the present section, we consider distributions that have a high likelihood of having generated the Ensemble sample. We were not surprised to see that the real return distribution of the Ensemble (and most countries) was skewed to the right. That is what one would expect if the distributions were approximately lognormal or log Student's t. We were surprised, however, to find that most of the $\log(1 + R)$ distributions, including that of the Ensemble, were skewed to the left. This suggested that we try some class of transformations that would have M_3 values between that of $(1 + R)$ and $\log(1 + R)$. The natural choice seemed

$$y_\alpha = (1 + r)^\alpha, \quad \alpha \in (0, 1) \tag{16}$$

since, on the one hand, $y_\alpha = (1 + r)$ when $\alpha = 1$ and, on the other hand, the M_3 and M_4 of y_α approach those of $\log(1 + r)$ as $\alpha \downarrow 0$.[5]

For the Ensemble, Table 5.6 presents the sample mean m, standard deviation σ, M_3, and M_4 of $y = \log(1 + r)$ and $(1 + r)^\alpha$ for various α. Sample M_3 was zero at $y = (1 + R)^{0.4}$. But when α was varied and m, σ, M_3, and M_4 were chosen so as to maximize LH for each α, the maximum of these maxima was at $\alpha = 0.5$. The first seven rows of Table 5.7 present information concerning the Ensemble's LH-maximizing solutions[6] for $y = \log(1 + R)$ and for $(1 + R)^\alpha$ for $\alpha = 0.1, 0.3, 0.5, 0.7, 0.9,$ and 1.0. The final two rows present the same information for the LH-maximizing lognormal and log Student's t distributions, respectively. The first column of the table identifies y; the second shows the maximum LLH of this y transformation; the next five columns show m, σ, M_3, and M_4 and the associated Pearson type for the transformed variables, such as the m, σ, M_3, and M_4 and type of $y = \log(1 + R)$. The final four columns show m, σ, M_3, and M_4 of the corresponding distribution of $(1 + R)$. For example, according to the next-to-last row of the table, the first four entries of that row show that the LH-maximizing normal distribution for $y = \log(1 + R)$ had $m = 0.05$, $\sigma = 0.22$, and of course, $M_3 = 0$ and $M_4 = 3$, whereas the corresponding distribution of $(1 + R)$, which is lognormal, had a mean of 1.078, a standard deviation of 0.25, $M_3 = 0.69$, and $M_4 = 3.87$.

TABLE 5.6 Ensemble Moments and Type of the Transformed Variables

	Arith. Mean	Std. Dev.	M_3	M_4	Pearson Type IV
$\log(1 + R)$	0.050	0.22	−1.20	14.92	X
$(1 + R)^{0.1}$	1.005	0.02	−0.82	11.55	X
$(1 + R)^{0.2}$	1.011	0.04	−0.50	9.37	X
$(1 + R)^{0.3}$	1.017	0.07	−0.24	8.00	X
$(1 + R)^{0.4}$	1.024	0.09	0.00	7.19	X
$(1 + R)^{0.5}$	1.031	0.11	0.21	6.77	X
$(1 + R)^{0.6}$	1.039	0.14	0.40	6.63	X
$(1 + R)^{0.7}$	1.048	0.16	0.58	6.72	X
$(1 + R)^{0.8}$	1.057	0.18	0.75	6.98	X
$(1 + R)^{0.9}$	1.066	0.21	0.92	7.39	X
$1 + R$	1.076	0.24	1.09	7.95	X

The LLH column of Table 5.7 shows little variation in LLH among the LH-maximizing distributions when y equals, alternately, $\log(1 + R)$ and $(1 + R)^\alpha$ for α from 0.1 to 1.0. The largest LLH is 91.87 for $y = (1 + R)^{1/2}$; the smallest is 91.22 for $y = (1 + R)^{0.1}$. Thus the largest Bayes factor among these distributions is $10^{0.65} = 4.47$. The Bayes factor is somewhat larger between the LH-maximizing $y = (1 + R)^{1/2}$ distribution, on the one hand, and the LH-maximizing Student's t distribution, on the other hand, with an LLH of 90.72, and therefore

TABLE 5.7 Moments, Pearson Types, and LLH for Various LLH-Maximizing Distributions

		Transformed Variables					$(1+r)$			
	LLH	Arith. Mean	Std. Dev.	M_3	M_4	Type	Arith. Mean	Std. Dev.	M_3	M_4
$\log(1+r)$	91.35	0.049	0.22	−0.57	21.70	IV	1.075	0.25	2.79	47.02
0.1	91.22	1.005	0.02	−0.49	18.27	IV	1.075	0.24	2.33	37.78
0.3	91.44	1.016	0.07	−0.14	17.02	IV	1.073	0.24	1.99	30.05
0.5	91.87	1.031	0.11	0.50	18.61	IV	1.076	0.24	2.02	27.43
0.7	91.83	1.048	0.16	0.85	20.10	IV	1.076	0.24	1.71	20.86
0.9	91.68	1.066	0.21	1.17	22.21	IV	1.076	0.24	1.45	15.83
$(1+r)$	91.56	1.075	0.24	1.33	23.93	IV	1.075	0.24	1.33	23.93
$\log(1+r)$	21.15	0.050	0.22	0.00	3.00	N	1.078	0.25	0.69	3.87
$\log(1+r)$	90.72	0.058	0.22	0.00	26.59	VII	1.086	0.26	3.85	63.74

with a Bayes factor between them of $10^{1.15} = 14.13$. The massive shift is between any of these and the LH-maximizing lognormal, that is, with $y = \log(1 + R)$ normally distributed. This has an LLH of about 21 and therefore a Bayes factor of about 10^{70} against it. This does not rule out the possibility that individual country distributions are lognormal, but the Ensemble definitely is not.

Figure 5.4 shows the cumulative distribution for $(1 + R)$ under four hypotheses, namely, for the LH-maximizing distributions such that

$y = \log(1 + R)$ is normally distributed.
$y = \log(1 + R)$ is distributed as Student's t.
$y = (1 + R)^{1/2}$ is some Pearson distribution.
$(1 + R)$ is some Pearson distribution.

The last three are quite close; the first (the lognormal) is different. In particular, one would not introduce much error if (because tabulations of the Student's t distributions are readily available) one decided to assume that $y = \log(1 + R)$ was Student's t with $M_4 = 26.6$ when in fact $y = (1 + R)^{1/2}$ was Type IV with $M_3 = 0.5$ and $M_4 = 18.6$.

TRANSFORMED COUNTRY DISTRIBUTIONS

As noted earlier, most $(1 + R)$ samples were skewed to the right, most $\log(1 + R)$ samples were skewed to the left, and the likelihood-maximizing hypothesis for the Ensemble was

FIGURE 5.4 Cumulative Distributions of Return Under Alternative Hypotheses.

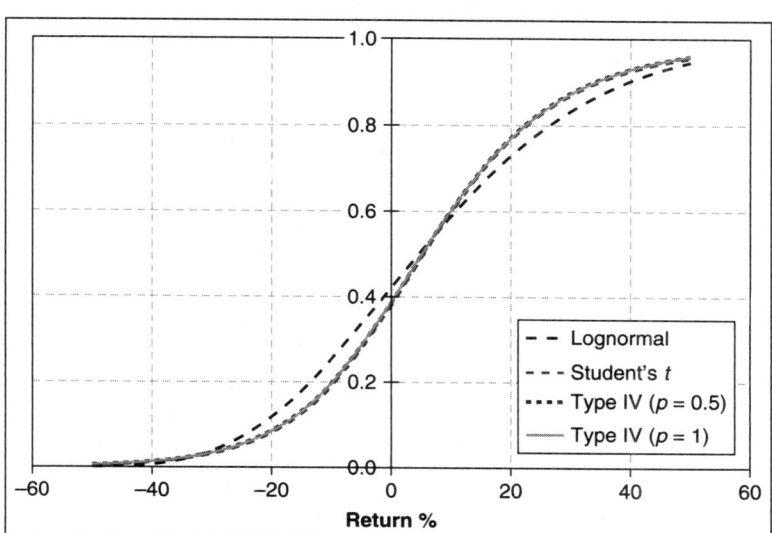

that $y = (1 + R)^{1/2}$ was some Pearson. This suggested that we compute M_3 and M_4 for $y = (1 + R)^\alpha$ with various values of α for the 19 country sample distributions. Doing so, we found that for $\alpha = 0.2$, the majority of distributions were skewed to the left, and for $\alpha = 0.3$, the majority were skewed to the right. At $\alpha = 0.25$, the split between left-skewed and right-skewed distributions was as even as possible: nine one way and ten the other.

Table 5.8 presents the arithmetic mean, standard deviation, M_3, M_4, and sample types for $y = (1 + R)^{0.25}$ for the 19 countries and the Ensemble. The M_3, M_4, and type information is presented in Figure 5.5. As the figure shows, not only does the $(1 + R)^{0.25}$ transformation split the sample as evenly

TABLE 5.8 Sample Moments and Pearson Types for $X = \log(1 + r)^{0.25}$

		Arith. Mean	Std. Dev.	M_3	M_4	Pearson Type		
						IV	I	VI
1	Australia	0.073	0.172	−0.750	3.643		x	
2	Belgium	0.029	0.213	0.099	3.319	x		
3	Canada	0.058	0.160	−0.327	2.927		x	
4	Denmark	0.050	0.169	0.849	5.680	x		
5	Finland	0.061	0.267	−0.189	4.912	x		
6	France	0.035	0.221	−0.077	2.635		x	
7	Germany	0.033	0.347	−2.961	24.474			x
8	Ireland	0.047	0.206	−0.244	4.648	x		
9	Italy	0.026	0.291	−0.961	6.806	x		
10	Japan	0.043	0.331	−2.285	14.738			x
11	Netherlands	0.056	0.187	0.274	3.907	x		
12	New Zealand	0.058	0.183	−0.552	8.658	x		
13	Norway	0.038	0.220	0.458	6.975	x		
14	South Africa	0.067	0.202	−0.101	5.109	x		
15	Spain	0.036	0.203	−0.023	3.677	x		
16	Sweden	0.063	0.202	−0.222	3.754	x		
17	Switzerland	0.046	0.182	−0.144	3.300	x		
18	United Kingdom	0.056	0.191	−0.797	7.517	x		
19	United States	0.067	0.195	−0.655	3.173		x	
20	Ensemble	0.050	0.225	−1.200	14.920	x		

FIGURE 5.5 Sample $(1 + R)^{0.25}$ and Pearson Boundaries.

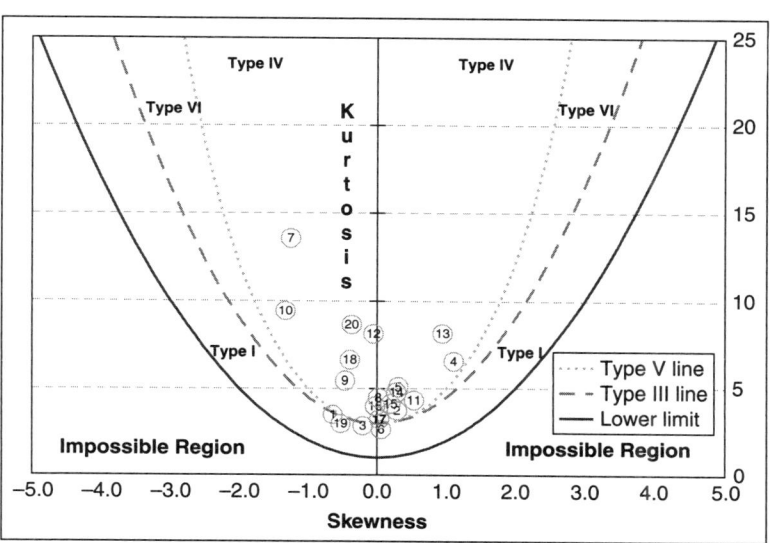

as possible between countries with $M_3 > 0$ and those with $M_3 < 0$, but it also tightens the extremes of M_3, as compared to those of the $y = (1 + R)$ and $y = \log(1 + R)$ samples. In particular, the $y = (1 + R)$ samples included M_3 values of as much as 2.58 (Norway), 1.98 (Denmark), and 1.51 (Germany), as well as two samples with $M_3 < 0$, whereas the $y = \log(1 + R)$ samples included M_3 values with negative extremes as low as -2.96 (Germany) and -2.29 (Japan), as well as distributions with positive M_3. For $(1 + R)^{0.25}$, the most negative M_3 were -1.34 (Japan) and -1.26 (Germany), and its highest positive M_3 are 1.11 (Denmark) and 0.95 (Norway). The range (max minus min) was 1.45 for $y = (1 + R)^{0.25}$ as compared to 2.82 for $y = (1 + R)$ and 3.81 for $y = \log(1 + R)$. In addition, the M_3 of the Ensemble was much closer to zero for its $y = (1 + R)^{0.25}$ than for its $y = (1 + R)$ or $\log(1 + R)$ samples: -0.37 for the first versus 1.09 and -1.20 for the latter two.

OBSERVATIONS[7]

Nontechnical discussions of possible gains or losses from a mean-variance efficient portfolio frequently assume that returns are normally distributed. The authors of this chapter were surprised to see that this was approximately true for twentieth-century real returns in Australia, Canada, and the United States. As Figure 5.1 shows, it was not true for most or all of the other country distributions. They have both higher M_3 and higher M_4. As we have seen, the effect of the former in shifting distributions to the right tends to dominate the effect of the latter in spreading out distributions as far as standard probability levels are concerned. For example, Table 5.5 shows that the Pearson distribution with $(M_3, M_4) = (1, 5)$ has 1 and 2.5 percent levels of 1.72 and 1.53 as compared to normal levels of 2.33 and 1.96.

Models used in options pricing and in the evaluation of new instruments often assume, with Black and Scholes, that return distributions are lognormal. Markowitz and Usmen show that, for daily moves on the S&P 500, a Bayesian would shift belief massively against that hypothesis in favor of the hypothesis that $\log(1 + R)$ is distributed as a Student's t distribution with between 4 and 5 degrees of freedom. One would expect, however, that annual returns would be closer to lognormal. If daily returns were independent and identically distributed (they're not, but if they were), the central limit theorem, applied to the sample's average log return rather than its average return, would imply that the log(1 + R) of annual returns would be near normal. Figure 5.2 shows that many countries did indeed have real annual return distributions whose log(1 + R) had (M_3, M_4) near (0, 3), consistent with the conclusion in Chapter 3 that, in the case of the DMS database, the best of the six approximations examined assumed that return distributions are lognormal. On the other hand, there were a good many exceptions, including Countries 7 (Germany) and 10 (Japan), whose log(1 + R) had M_4 much larger than 3 and had negative M_3, as did (to a lesser extent) Countries 9 (Italy), 12 (New Zealand), and 18 (United Kingdom). Since negative skewness especially, and to a certain extent high kurtosis, pushes probability into the left tail, a lognormal assumption would have been too optimistic for these countries.

We think of (1 + R) and log(1 + R) as random variables defined on some sample space. A class of random variables intermediate between these two are those of the form $y = (1 + R)^\alpha$ for $\alpha \in (0, 1)$. In this connection, we found that, among the hypotheses considered, the LH-maximizing hypothesis for the Ensemble was a Type IV distribution for $(1 + R)^{1/2}$, and that the $(1 + R)^{1/4}$ transformation applied to the individual country returns resulted in distributions that were divided as equally as possible between negative and positive M_3.

It seems to us improbable that, in the next hundred years, the German and Japanese equity markets will experience the losses they saw at the end of World War II. A century is a long time, of course, and the world could change a great deal in the course of a century, as it did during the twentieth century. The equities of some countries might very well experience great real losses. But there is no particular reason that we can see to suppose that this would happen again specifically to Germany or Japan. This suggests that a type of hypothesis worth exploring is that, in any long stretch of years (like a century), one or more countries' equity markets will have sample return distributions that could not reasonably have come from a lognormal distribution. But it won't necessarily be the same countries each time.

RECOMMENDATION

We argued throughout this volume that, for a wide variety of risk-averse investors, *if* the investor can choose a portfolio from an efficient frontier that best serves his, her, or its needs, *then* the investor will have approximately maximized the expected utility. The problem this statement bypasses is how to choose this right-for-the-investor portfolio. One way that is often used is to show the investor the likelihoods of various downside moves, as well as the expected returns of selected portfolios. Another is to use Monte Carlo simulation to estimate the likelihoods of possible long-run consequences of decisions such as savings rate, retirement age, and portfolio choice. Both these approaches require return distributions.

Ideally, the organization that generates an efficient frontier should estimate its return distribution. The broad outline of a process to do so is straightforward:

1. Select representative portfolios from the frontier.
2. For each representative portfolio, compute a return series for the portfolio (for example, from the return series of its constituents) to serve as a sample from the portfolio's return distribution.
3. Perform an analysis (for example, like the one we did for the Ensemble) to find maximum LH and near-maximum LH distributions that might well have generated the sample.

From the distributions identified in Step 3, chose one to serve as "the" distribution for the portfolio.

Needless to say, this is easier said than done. At this level of abstraction, the computing of an efficient frontier is also "straightforward": make estimates; choose constraints; compute frontier. Those who have gone through the process of constructing efficient frontiers know that a conscientious effort to do so involves a myriad of challenging subtasks, such as deciding which securities or asset classes to include; which historical series to use for initial estimates; which statistical procedures to apply to these series; which adjustments to make as forward-looking estimates to reflect "the current situation" (such as the low-interest-rate environment as this is written); which factor model of covariance, if any, to use; how to fashion constraints to represent objectives other than portfolio mean and variance (such as liquidity and turnover constraints); and the like. Some of these subtasks—such as the development of return series for mean and covariance estimates, and perhaps the decision to use a factor model of covariance—could feed into the process of estimating the form of the return distribution. Granted, estimating a return distribution is not an easy matter. The alternatives are to not offer the investors return distributions or to pick the distributions out of the air with no empirical support.

NOTES

Chapter 1

1. If Outcome 4 is preferred to Outcome 2, then there is a probability q such that a probability of q of getting Outcome 4 and a probability $(1 - q)$ of getting Outcome 1 is exactly as good as Outcome 2 with certainty. Hence:

$$u_2 = qu_4 + (1-q)u_1$$

that is,

$$1 = qu_4$$
$$u_4 = \frac{1}{q}$$

Finally, if Outcome 1 is preferred to Outcome 5, then there is an r such that a probability r of Outcome 2 versus $(1 - r)$ of Outcome 5 is exactly as good as certainty of Outcome 1. Hence

$$u_1 = ru_2 + (1-r)u_5$$

that is,

$$0 = r + (1-r)u_5$$
$$u_5 = \frac{-r}{1-r}$$

Thus, once the zero and the unit are chosen, the utilities attached to other outcomes follow from the individual's preferences.

2. Concerning Weber's Law generally, see, for example, "Weber's law," *Encyclopedia Online* (Chicago: Encyclopedia Britannica, Inc., 2012), http://www.britannica.com/EBchecked/topic/638610/Webers-law; accessed June 13, 2012. Kontek applies Weber's Law to prize size. If instead one applied it to end-of-period wealth, one would obtain the Bernoulli (1954) [1738] log-wealth utility function. Thus the Bernoulli utility, postulated before Weber's time, may be viewed as Weber's Law applied to one's perception of affluence.

3. More generally, Markowitz (1952), footnote 10, claims and Markowitz (2010) demonstrates that an expected utility maximizer would never prefer a multiple-prize lottery to all single-prize lotteries with a given expected loss (for example, equal to zero for a "fair" lottery). C in the text is essentially a multiple-prize lottery—with two win and one "loss" possible outcomes—whereas A and B each have one win and one loss possible outcomes.

Chapter 2

1. More generally, if a probability distribution is joint elliptical, then EU is a function of mean and variance. See Chamberlain (1983).

2. In addition to implying risk-averse behavior—preferring certainty to a gamble with equal or less expected return—the expected values of concave functions also

have the property that a local maximum is always a global maximum; that is, if some set of parameter values, $X_1 = X_1^0, X_2 = X_2^0, \ldots, X_n = X_n^0$, has a greater value of EU than do any nearby values of $X_1, X_2, \ldots, X_n$, then there is no distant set of values $X_1 = X_1^*, X_2 = X_2^*, \ldots, X_n = X_n^*$, that gives a still greater value of EU. This greatly reduces computational time for maximizing EU.

3. In the financial literature, $(1 + R)$ is sometimes called "return," with R itself being called "rate of return." Also, $(1 + R)$ is sometimes referred to as wealth, that is, end-of-period wealth, W_{t+1}, scaled so that beginning-of-period wealth, W_t, is 1. These various usages are equivalent, as long as they are used consistently in any one context. We will refer to R as either return or rate of return interchangeably, since common English does speak of either a 6 percent return or a 6 percent rate of return. We refer to $(1 + R)$ as "one plus return."

Chapter 3

1. One maximizes real growth if and only if one also maximizes nominal growth, since real return (R_R) satisfies

$$1 + R_R = (1 + R)/(1 + I) \qquad (\mathbf{N1})$$

where I is the rate of inflation. Thus the real growth rate (g_R) satisfies

$$\begin{aligned} \log(1 + g_R) &= E \log(1 + R_R) \\ &= E \log(1 + R) - E \log(1 + g_I) \qquad (\mathbf{N2}) \end{aligned}$$

where $1 + g_I$ is the geometric mean of the $(1 + I)$ distribution. Therefore,

$$1 + g_R = (1 + g)/(1 + g_I) \tag{N3}$$

Since Equation (N2) holds whether I is constant or random and, in the latter case, whether or not R and I are correlated, the same is true for Equation (N3): one plus the real growth rate equals one plus the nominal growth rate divided by one plus the inflation rate, which implies that the assertion is proven.

2. For example, for $\log(1 + R)$ normally distributed with mean μ and standard deviation σ, Stuart and Ord (1994), Exercise 2.30, implies that

$$E(1 + R) = \exp\left[\mu + \frac{1}{2}\sigma^2\right]$$
$$E(1 + R)^2 = \exp(2\mu + 2\sigma^2)$$

From this follows

$$\log(1 + E) = \mu + \frac{1}{2}\sigma^2$$
$$\log(V + (1 + E)^2) = 2\mu + 2\sigma^2$$

Thus

$$\mu = E\log(1 + R)$$
$$= 2\log(1 + E) - \frac{1}{2}\log[V + (1 + E)^2]$$

Therefore,

$$1 + g = \exp[E \log(1 + R)]$$
$$= (1 + E)^2/\sqrt{V + (1 + E)^2}$$

Hence Equation (10e).

3. Jean and Helms cite Latané (1959). Whereas Latané discusses the two-outcome case, we do not find Equation (10f) in this reference. We do find it in Latané and Tuttle (1967) with a different justification.

4. Since $\sigma / (1 + E) \to 0$ as $E \to \infty$ for fixed σ, we have $X << 0.93$ asymptotically, and the ordering in inequalities (17) holds. Therefore, to prove the assertion in the text, it is sufficient to show that

$$\lim_{E \to \infty} (E - g_{EDD}) = 0 \tag{N1}$$

(See Figure 3.2.) Limit (N1) holds if and only if

$$\lim_{E \to \infty} [(1 + E) - (1 + g_{EDD})] = 0 \tag{N2}$$

But this limit is of the form

$$\lim[g(x) - f(x)] = 0 \tag{N3}$$

which holds if and only if

$$\lim\left[1 - \frac{f(x)}{g(x)}\right] = 0 \tag{N4}$$

provided that $g(x)$ does not approach zero. Limit (N4) is equivalent to the following two limits:

$$\frac{f(x)}{g(x)} \to 1 \tag{N5}$$

$$\log[f(x)] - \log[g(x)] \to 0 \tag{N6}$$

But Equation (15b) implies that

$$\Delta = \log(1 + g_{\text{EDD}}) - \log(1 + E)$$
$$= -\frac{1}{2}Y - \frac{3}{4}Y^2$$

For a given V, $Y \to 0$ as $E \to \infty$; therefore, $\Delta \to 0$, and the assertion in the text follows.

5. A comment by Markowitz (1952a) could easily be interpreted that way.

6. Some numbers from the source of Table 3.4 in this chapter differ slightly from the corresponding numbers reported in Chapters 4 and 5, computed directly from the DMS database. For example, the arithmetic mean of Australia is 9.0 here and 9.2 as reported in Chapters 4 and 5. Also, the source of Table 3.4 in the present chapter reports Swiss real equity returns from 1911, whereas that for Chapters 4 and 5 reports the same from 1900. We recomputed Tables 3.4, 3.5, and 3.6 using the DMS database and found that the differences were inconsequential. For example, in the last line of Table 3.4, "Nr. times best" (or tied for best), the number of times

QE was best or tied for best increased from 7 to 8, while that for LMT fell from 2 to 0. There were no further changes in these counts. Since the time we promised to deliver this volume to the publisher was fast approaching when these recomputations were performed, and we would have had to rewrite the details of the text if we had switched tables, we decided to leave the tables as originally computed from Dimson et al. (2002).

Chapter 4

1. We refer here to semivariance around the expected value E rather than semivariance around some fixed value b, such as $b = 0$. The former seems to us likely to fit better than the latter, based on the results reported in the previous chapter showing that the quadratic fit about E does much better than that about zero. Further explorations along the lines of this paper could try it both ways with various settings of b.

Chapter 5

1. **Anthony Tessitore** is managing director and portfolio manager at Gramercy Funds Management LLC, Greenwich, Connecticut. **Ansel Tessitore** is a math major, class of 2014, at Bates College, Lewiston, Maine. **Nilufer Usmen** is a professor of finance at Montclair State University, Montclair, New Jersey.
2. This statement is qualified later, in the section "Compound Hypotheses."

3. In choosing among several models with differing numbers (k) of parameters, Akaike recommends choosing the one that minimizes AIC (Akaike information criteria):

$$\text{AIC} = -2\log[\text{LH}(\hat{\theta})] + 2k$$

where $\hat{\theta}$ is the LH-maximizing value of the model's parameter vector θ. Schwarz shows that, under certain assumptions, the log posterior probability of a model M given a sample S is

$$\log P(\text{model}|S) = \log[\text{LH}(\tilde{\theta})] - \frac{1}{2}k\log n + R$$

where the remainder R remains bounded as $n \to \infty$. Markowitz and Usmen point out difficulties with the Akaike and Schwarz criteria. Alparslan et al. recommend as a Bayes factor the ratio of terms of the form

$$(2\pi)^{k/2} |\hat{H}|^{1/2} \text{LH}(\hat{\theta})$$

where $\hat{H}$ is the negative inverse Hessian of the log-likelihood function evaluated at $\hat{\theta}$.

4. The following relationships apply to two types of situations: (1) when y is drawn from a distribution that itself has been randomly generated by a "generating distribution," or (2) rather than a generating distribution, the probabilities associated with specific ("generated") distributions are the subjective beliefs of some Bayesian decision maker. As noted in the text, we will denote

by E_H and V_H, for example, the mean and variance of x given H. Then:

$$E(y) = E(E_H)$$

The E without subscript on the right in the previous equation is the expected value over all hypotheses H. (In some cases that follow, the E operator represents an overall expected value, that is, the expected value over all hypotheses of the expected value given the hypothesis. The meaning of E should be clear from context.) In what follows we write $\bar{E}$ for $E(y)$. The variance of y is:

$$\begin{aligned} V(y) &= E(y - \bar{E})^2 \\ &= E(y - E_H + E_H - \bar{E})^2 \\ &= E(y - E_H)^2 + E(E_H - \bar{E})^2 + 2E(y - E_H)(E_H - \bar{E}) \end{aligned}$$

But the third term on the right is zero, since $E(y - E_H)$ is zero for each H; therefore

$$V(y) = E(y - E_H)^2 + V(E_H)$$

Thus for a Bayesian, the appropriate estimate for the variance of a random variable is *not* its most likely V_H or its average V_H, but the latter plus the variance of E_H. Similarly,

$$\begin{aligned} E(y - \bar{E})^3 &= E(y - E_H + E_H - \bar{E})^3 \\ &= E(y - E_H)^3 + E(E_H - \bar{E})^3 + 3E(y - E_H) \\ &\quad (E_H - \bar{E})^2 + 3E(y - E_H)^2 (E_H - \bar{E}) \end{aligned}$$

In this case, the third term on the right, but not the fourth, is necessarily zero. If we make the simplifying assumption that the variance of y given H is uncorrelated with $(E_H - \overline{E})$, then the third central moment of y is the average (over all H) of the third moment $E(y - E_H)^3$ plus the third central moment of the E_H. Finally,

$$E(y - \overline{E})^4 = E(y - E_H + E_H - \overline{E})^4$$
$$= E(y - E_H)^4 + E(E_H - \overline{E})^4 + 4E(y - E_H)$$
$$(E_H - \overline{E})^3 + 4E(y - E_H)^3 (E_H - \overline{E})$$
$$+ 6E(y - E_H)^2 (E_H - \overline{E})^2$$

Again, the third term on the right, but not the fourth, is necessarily zero. If we add the simplifying assumption that the second and third central moments of y given H are independent of $(E_H - \overline{E})$, then we have

$$E(y - \overline{E})^4 = E(y - E_H)^4 + E(E_H - \overline{E})^4 + 6EV_H \cdot V(E_H)$$

The M_3 and M_4 of y are defined in terms of these central moments.

5. Stuart and Ord, Section 2.6.
6. Our parameterization of the Pearson Type IV probability density follows Nagahara (1999) and is given by

$$p(x|u, t, d, b) = \frac{C \exp\left[2bd \tan^{-1}\left(\frac{x-u}{t}\right)\right]}{[(x-u)^2 + t^2]^b}$$

where u, t, b, and d are real-valued parameters, $b > \frac{1}{2}$, $t > 0$, and C is the normalizing constant. The Pearson

Type IV density is an asymmetric Student's t (it becomes Student's t density when $d = 0$). The normalizing constant C is given by the following formula:

$$C = \frac{\Gamma(b + bdi)\Gamma(b - bdi)}{\Gamma(b)^2} \frac{t^{2b-1}}{B(b - \frac{1}{2}, \frac{1}{2})}$$

where $\Gamma(x)$ and $B(x)$ are the complex gamma and beta functions, respectively. To compute the normalizing constant, we used the following formula from Abramowitz and Stegun (1965) as cited in Heinrich (2004) and Nagahara (1999):

$$\frac{\Gamma(b + bdi)\Gamma(b - bdi)}{\Gamma(b)^2} = \prod_{n=0}^{\infty} \frac{1}{\{1 + [(bd)^2/(b + n)^2]\}}$$

The series converged rapidly for all parameter values of b and d considered in this study. Our computation was based on 1 million terms, but the gain in precision with more than 100,000 terms was negligible (10^{-9}).

Return observations were assumed to be independent and identically distributed. Thus, given T observations, $x^1, x^2, \ldots, x_T$, the log-likelihood is given by:

$$\text{LLH}(u, t, d, b) = \sum_{t=1}^{T} \log C + 2bd \sum_{t=1}^{T} \tan^{-1}\left(\frac{x_t - u}{t}\right)$$
$$- b\sum_{t=1}^{T} \log[(x_t - u)^2 + t^2]$$

These equations form the basis of the models considered in this study.

We obtained parameters u, t, d, and b by maximizing the log-likelihood function just given. Searches were conducted numerically, in parameter space, using a sampling procedure that is further explained later. Given the history, $x_1, x_2, \ldots, x_T$, we computed sample moments and parameter values associated with those moments. Moments were converted to parameters using the following equations:

$$r \equiv 2(b-1) = \frac{6(\beta_2 - \beta_1 - 1)}{2\beta_2 - 3\beta_1 - 6};$$

$$-2bd = \frac{r(r-2)\sqrt{\beta_1}}{\sqrt{16(r-1) - \beta_1(r-2)^2}}$$

$$t = \frac{\sqrt{\mu_2[16(r-1) - \beta_1(r-2)^2]}}{4};$$

$$u = \mu_1 - \frac{(r-2)\sqrt{\beta_1}\sqrt{\mu_2}}{4}$$

where $\mu_1, \mu_2, \sqrt{\beta_1}$, and β_2 are *mean, variance, skewness,* and *kurtosis* of the data series. These equations are from Heinrich (2004) with symbols adopted from Nagahara (1999). The inverse relation, expressing moments in terms of parameters and the restrictions on these parameters, is given by the following:

$$\mu_1 = \frac{bdt}{b-1} + u \ (1 < b)$$

$$\mu_2 = \frac{t^2}{2b-3}\left[1 + \left(\frac{bd}{b-1}\right)^2\right] (\tfrac{3}{2} < b)$$

$$\sqrt{\beta_1} = \frac{2bdt}{(b-1)(b-2)}\mu_2^{-1/2} \ (2 < b)$$

$$\beta_2 = \frac{3t^2}{(2b-5)}\left[1 + \frac{b+2}{b-1}\left(\frac{bd}{b-1}\right)^2\right]\mu_2^{-1} \ (\tfrac{5}{2} < b)$$

The method for estimating the parameters requires maximizing the log-likelihood function and was done numerically. The optimization process randomly sampled volumes from parameter space and evaluated LLH at every sampled point. The approach was used because the likelihood function might not be concave, and a gradient search might have stalled around a local maximum. In the procedure, we first constructed a "rectangle" in parameter space that was 50 percent above and 50 percent below the sample parameter values in each dimension. Second, LLH was calculated on randomly selected points within that volume (the "50 percent box"). Specifically, 100,000 randomly selected points within that rectangle were used. The maximizing parameters from this initial search were selected, and a second "40 percent box" was created and centered on the maximizing parameters. Again using 100,000 randomly selected points within the "40 percent box," LLH was maximized. Next, around the latest maximizing parameters, a "30 percent box" was created. The process was continued down to the final 5 percent box centered on the optimal point from the prior search. Continuing the process past this stage produced negligible improvement in LLH. At the end of this search procedure, the maximum LLH values, parameters, and moments were reported.

For a few of our optimizations, we tried following our sampling approach with a gradient search, starting with the best solution we had found. The largest improvement that the gradient search found over our prior best was LLH = 91.5656, as compared to our previous 91.5650. We therefore discontinued the use of the gradient tack-on procedure and report only the results of the sampling procedure.

7. As we noted in the introduction to this chapter, it was beyond the scope of the project reported here to have performed a Bayesian analysis comparable to that of Markowitz and Usmen for daily moves in the S&P 500 or our analysis of the Ensemble, as described in the previous endnote, for each of the 19 countries. Thus the text here compares standard assumptions about distributions with sample distributions, that is, the empirical distributions that investors would have experienced for the particular countries through the twentieth century.

REFERENCES

Abramowitz, M., and I. A. Stegun (1965). *Handbook of Mathematical Functions*. New York: Dover.

Akaike, H. (1974). "A New Look at the Statistical Model Identification." *IEEE Transactions on Automatic Control* AO-19:716–723.

——— (1977). "Entropy Maximization Principle." In *Applications of Statistics*, edited by P. R. Krishnaiah, 27–41. Amsterdam: North-Holland Publishing Co.

——— (1979). "A Bayesian Extension of the Minimum AIC Procedure of Autoregressive Model Fitting." *Biometrika* 66:237–242.

Allais, M. (1953). "Le Comportement de l'Homme Rationnel Devant le Risque: Critique des Postulats et Axiomes de l'Ecole Americaine." *Econometrica* 21(4):503–546.

Alparslan, A., A. Tessitore, and N. Usmen (2013). "Stable Paretian vs. Student's *t* Stock Market Hypothesis. *Journal of Statistical Theory and Practice* 7(1):133–145.

Arnott, R. D., and P. Bernstein (2002). "What Risk Premium Is Normal?" *Financial Analysts Journal* 58(2):64–85.

Bellman, R. E. (1957). *Dynamic Programming*. Princeton, NJ: Princeton University Press.

Bernoulli, Daniel (1954). *Specimen Theoriae Novae de Mensura Sortis* [Exposition of a New Theory on the Measurement of Risk], translated by Louise Sommer. *Econometrica* 22:23–26. [Originally published in *Commentarii Academiae Scientiarum Imperialis Petropolitanae* 5:175–192 (1738).]

Black, F., and R. Litterman (1991). "Asset Allocation: Combining Investor Views with Market Equilibrium." *Journal of Fixed Income* 1(2):7–18.

Black, F., and M. Scholes (1973). "The Pricing of Options and Corporate Liabilities." *Journal of Political Economy* 81(3):637–654.

Breiman, L. (1960). "Investment Policies for Expanding Businesses Optimal in a Long Run Sense." *Naval Research Logistics Quarterly* 7(4):647–651.

Brinson, G. P., L. R. Hood, and G. L. Beebower (1986). "Determinants of Portfolio Performance." *Financial Analysts Journal* 42(4):39–44.

Brinson, G. P., B. D. Singer, and G. L. Beebower (1991). "Determinants of Portfolio Performance II: An Update." *Financial Analysts Journal* 47(3):40–48.

Chamberlain, G. (1983). "A Characterization of the Distributions That Imply Mean-Variance Utility Functions." *Journal of Economic Theory* 29(1):185–210.

De Finetti, B. (1937). "La Prévision: Ses Lois Logiques, Ses Sources Subjectives." *Annals de l'Institute Henri Poincaré* 7. English translation in *Studies in Subjective Probability*, edited by H. E. Kyburg, Jr., and H. G. Smokler (1964). New York: John Wiley & Sons.

Descartes, R. D. (1968). "First Meditation." *Meditations and Other Metaphysical Writings*, translated by M. Clarke. New York: Penguin Classics. (First published in 1641.)

Dexter, A. S., J. N. W. Yu, and W. T. Ziemba (1980). "Portfolio Selection in a Lognormal Market When the Investor Has a Power Utility Function: Computational Results." In *Stochastic Programming*, edited by M. A. H. Dempster, 507–523. New York: Academic Press.

Dimson, E., P. Marsh, and M. Staunton (2002). *Triumph of the Optimists: 101 Years of Global Investment Returns.* Princeton, NJ: Princeton University Press.

Ederington, L. H. (1995). "Mean-Variance as an Approximation to Expected Utility Maximization: Semi Ex-Ante Results." In *Advances in Financial Economics*, Vol. 1, edited by Mark Hirschey and Wayne Marr. Oxford, UK: Pergamon.

Ellsberg, D. (1961). "Risk, Ambiguity and the Savage Axioms." *Quarterly Journal of Economics* 75(4):643–669.

Fernholz, R., and B. Shay (1982). "Stochastic Portfolio Theory and Stock Market Equilibrium." *Journal of Finance* 27(2):615–624.

Fishburn, P. C. (1982). *The Foundations of Expected Utility*. Boston: D. Reidel Publishing Co., Kluwer.

Grauer, R. R. (1986). "Normality, Solvency, and Portfolio Choice." *Journal of Financial and Quantitative Analysis* 21(3):265–278.

Hakansson, N. H. (1971). "Capital Growth and the Mean-Variance Approach to Portfolio Selection." *Journal of Financial and Quantitative Analysis* 6:517–577.

Hardy, G., J. E. Littlewood, and G. Pólya (1999). *Inequalities*, 2nd ed. Cambridge, UK: Cambridge Mathematical Library, Cambridge University Press.

Heinrich, J. (2004). *A Guide to the Pearson Type IV Distribution*. CDF/Memo/Statistics, University of Pennsylvania.

Hildreth, C. (1963). "Bayesian Statisticians and Remote Clients." *Econometrica* 31:422–438.

Hlawitschka, W. (1994). "The Empirical Nature of Taylor-Series Approximations to Expected Utility." *American Economic Review* 84(3):713–719.

Hume, D. (1962). *A Treatise of Human Nature Book 1: Of the Understanding*. London: William Collins Sons & Co. Ltd. (First published in 1739.)

Ibbotson Stocks, Bonds, Bills, and Inflation (SBBI) Classic Yearbook (2010). Chicago: Morningstar, Inc.

Jean, W. H., and B. P. Helms (1983). "Geometric Mean Approximations." *Journal of Financial and Quantitative Analysis* 19(3):287–293.

Johnson, N. L., E. Nixon, and D. E. Amos (1963). "Table of Percentage Points of Pearson Curves, for Given $\sqrt{\beta_1}$ and β_2, Expressed in Standard Measure." *Biometrika* 50(3 & 4):459–498.

Jorion, P. (1997). *Value at Risk*. Chicago: R. D. Irwin.

Kahneman, D., and A. Tversky (1979). "Prospect Theory: An Analysis of Decision Under Risk." *Econometrica* 47(2):263–291.

Kaplan, P. D. (2012). *Frontiers of Modern Asset Allocation*. Hoboken, NJ: John Wiley & Sons.

Konno, H., and H. Yamazaki (1991). "Mean-Absolute Deviation Portfolio Optimization Model and Its Applications to Tokyo Stock Market." *Management Science* 37(5):519–531.

Kontek, K. (2011). "On Mental Transformations." *Journal of Neuroscience, Psychology and Economics* 4(4):235–253.

Kritzman, M., S. Myrgren, and S. Page (2009). "Optimal Rebalancing: A Scalable Solution." *Journal of Investment Management* 7(1): 9–19.

Kroll, Y., H. Levy, and H. M. Markowitz (1984). "Mean Variance Versus Direct Utility Maximization." *Journal of Finance* 39(1):47–61.

Latané, H. A. (1959). "Criteria for Choice Among Risky Ventures." *Journal of Political Economy* 67(2):144–155.

Latané, H. A., and D. L. Tuttle (1967). "Criteria for Portfolio Building." *Journal of Finance* 22(3):359–373.

Levy, H., and H. M. Markowitz (1979). "Approximating Expected Utility by a Function of Mean and Variance." *American Economic Review* 69(3):308–317.

Loistl, O. (1976). "The Erroneous Approximation of Expected Utility by Means of a Taylor's Series Expansion: Analytic and Computational Results." *American Economic Review* 66(5):904–910.

Mandelbrot, B. (1963). "The Variation of Certain Speculative Prices." *Journal of Business* 36:394–419.

Markowitz, H. M. (1952a). "Portfolio Selection." *Journal of Finance* 7(1):77–91.

Markowtiz, H.M. (1952b). "The Utility of Wealth." *Journal of Political Economy* 152-158.

———— (1959). *Portfolio Selection: Efficient Diversification of Investments.* New York: John Wiley & Sons; 2nd ed. Cambridge, MA: Basil Blackwell, 1991.

———— (1987). *Mean-Variance Analysis in Portfolio Choice and Capital Markets.* Cambridge, MA: Basil Blackwell.

———— (1991a). "Foundations of Portfolio Theory." *Journal of Finance* 46(2):469–477.

———— (1991b). "Individual Versus Institutional Investing." *Financial Services Review* 1:1–8.

———— (1997). "On Socks, Ties and Extended Outcomes." In *Economic and Environmental Risk and Uncertainty*: *New Models and Methods*, edited by Nau et al., 219–226. Dordrecht, Netherlands: Kluwer Academic Publishers.

———— (2010). "Portfolio Theory: As I Still See It." *Annual Review of Financial Economics* 2:1–23.

———— (2012a). "Mean-Variance Approximations to the Geometric Mean." *Annals of Financial Economics* 7(1): 1250001 (30 pages).

———— (2012b). "The 'Great Confusion' Concerning MPT." *International Journal of Finance* 4:8–27.

Markowitz, H. M., D. W. Reid, and B. V. Tew (1994). "The Value of a Blank Check." *Journal of Portfolio Management* 20(4):82–91.

Markowitz, H. M., and P. Todd (2000). *Mean-Variance Analysis in Portfolio Choice and Capital Markets.* New Hope, PA: Frank Fabozzi and Associates. Reissue of Markowitz (1987) with chapter by P. Todd.

Markowitz, H. M., and N. Usmen (1996a). "The Likelihood of Various Stock Market Return Distributions, Part 1: Principles of Inference." *Journal of Risk and Uncertainty* 13:207–219.

———— (1996b). "The Likelihood of Various Stock Market Return Distributions, Part 2: Empirical Results." *Journal of Risk and Uncertainty* 13:221–247.

———— (2003). "Resampled Frontiers Versus Diffuse Bayes: An Experiment." *Journal of Investment Management* 1(4):9–25.

Markowitz, H. M., and E. van Dijk (2003). "Single-Period Mean-Variance Analysis in a Changing World." *Financial Analysts Journal* 59(2):30–44.

Markowitz, H. M., and G. Xu (1994). "Data Mining Corrections." *Journal of Portfolio Management* 21(1):60–69.

Marschak, J. (1950). "Rational Behavior, Uncertain Prospects, and Measurable Utility." *Econometrica* 18(2):

Menger, K. (1967. [1934]). "The Role of Uncertainty in Economics." In *Essays in Mathematical Economics in Honor of Oskar Morgenstern*, edited by M. Shubik. Princeton, NJ: Princeton University Press.

Michaud, R. O. (1998). *Efficient Asset Management: A Practical Guide to Stock Portfolio Optimization and Asset Allocation.* Boston: Harvard Business School Press.

Mossin, J. (1966). "Equilibrium in a Capital Asset Market." *Econometrica* 34(2):768–783.

Mossin, J. (1968), "Optimal Multiperiod Portfolio Policies." *Journal of Business*, 1(2), pp 215–229.

Nagahara, Y. (1999). "The PDF and CF of Pearson Type IV Distributions and the ML Estimation of the Parameters." *Elsevier Statistics & Probability Letters* 43:251–264.

Pulley, L. M. (1983). "Mean-Variance Approximations to Expected Logarithmic Utility." *Operations Research* 31(4):685–696.

Quiggin, J. (1993). *Generalized Expected Utility Theory.* Boston: Kluwer Academic Publishers. Third printing 1998.

Savage, L. J. (1954). *The Foundations of Statistics*, 2nd rev. ed. Dover, NY: John Wiley & Sons.

Schwarz, G. (1978). "Estimating the Dimension of a Model." *Annals of Statistics* 6:461–464.

Sharpe, W. F., and L. G. Tint (1990). "Liabilities—A New Approach." *Journal of Portfolio Management* 16(2):5–10.

Simaan, Y. (1993). "What Is the Opportunity Cost of Mean-Variance Investment Strategies?" *Management Science* 39(5):578–587.

Sortino, F., and S. Satchell (2001). *Managing Downside Risk in Financial Markets: Theory, Practice and Implementation*. Burlington, MA: Butterworth-Heinemann.

Stuart, A., and K. Ord (1994). *Kendall's Advanced Theory of Statistics*, Vol. 1: *Distribution Theory*, 6th ed. London: Edward Arnold.

Sun, W., A. Fan, L. W. Chen, T. Schouwenaars, and M. A. Albota (2006). "Optimal Rebalancing for Institutional Portfolios." *Journal of Portfolio Management* 32(2):33–43.

Von Neumann, J., and O. Morgenstern (1944). *Theory of Games and Economic Behavior*, 3rd ed. (1953). Princeton, NJ: Princeton University Press.

Wiesenberger, A., and Company (1941). *Investment Companies*. New York: Annual editions since 1941.

Young, W. E., and R. H. Trent (1969). "Geometric Mean Approximation of Individual Security and Portfolio Performance." *Journal of Financial Quantitative Analysis* 44:179–199.

INDEX

Absolute safety-first, 29
Adjusted MAD-squared, 128
   DMS database and, 140
   RMSQ and, 129–130
Adjusted semivariance, 128, 129
   SV and, 131–133
Adjusted VaR estimated variance
   RVEV, 133–135
   for 16 equity markets in twentieth century, 146
Adjusted variance
   arithmetic mean and, 132, 133
   DMS database and, 140
   geometric mean and, 129, 132, 133
   Taylor series approximations and, 129
AIC. *See* Akaike information criteria
Akaike, H., 160, 202
Akaike information criteria (AIC), 202
Allais, Maurice, 17
Allais's paradox, 17–24
   Axiom II and, 28
   HDMs and, 28
   RDMs and, 28
   Weber's Law and, 21–24
Alparslan, A.A., 160, 168
   RDMs and, 150–151
Annual returns, 51–53
   of asset classes, 169
   DMS database and, 191
   for mutual funds, 49, 50

Approximation errors
   arithmetic mean and, 85–86
   geometric mean and, 84–90
   MV and, 84–90
   standard deviation and, 85–88, 100
Arithmetic mean, 75
   geometric mean and, 118
   maximum loss and, 104–105
   MV and, 77–80
   for Pearson distributions, 170–172
Asset classes
   annual returns of, 169
   database, 124–127
Average absolute error of approximation, 82, 86
Average error of approximation, 82, 86
Axiom I
   bounded utility function and, 32
   EU, 25–26
Axiom II
   bounded utility function and, 32
   EU, 26–28
Axiom III
   bounded utility function and, 32
   EU, 28–29
   utility of returns and, 31

218 · Index

Axiom III'
   bounded utility function
      and, 2
   EU, 28–29
   utility of returns and, 31

Bayes factors, 151, 153–156
   compound hypotheses and,
      159–161
   LH and, 156
   LLH and, 186
   Pearson distributions and, 151,
      161–169
   posterior beliefs and, 154
   RDMs and, 153
   simple hypotheses
      and, 160
Bayes' rule, 151
Bayesian decision makers,
   151, 168
   belief ratio of, 154
   generated distributions
      and, 202
   variance and, 203
Belief ratio, 165
   of Bayesian decision
      makers, 154
   LH and, 155
   with simple hypotheses, 159
Beliefs. *See also* Posterior beliefs
   PB, 151–152
Bernoulli, Daniel, 33
Bernoulli utility, 196
Beta distributions of first
   kind, 173
Black-Scholes financial model,
   113, 190
Bounded utility function, 34
Bounded utility of returns,
   31–34

Call options, 58–63
Cauchy distributions, 162
Certainty-equivalent
   wealth, 70
Chi-squared distributions, 151
Coffee
   without cream, 27
   without milk, 27
Coins. *See* Flipping coins
Compound hypotheses
   Bayes factors and, 159–161
   normal distributions
      and, 167
   Pearson distributions
      and, 168
Concave utility curve
   for level of return, 12, 13
   MV and, 69
   RDMs and, 14
   risk-aversion and, 14, 69, 149,
      196–197
Conditional value at risk
   (CVaR), 124, 127. *See also*
   CVaR-squared
   DMS database and, 140
   geometric mean and, 135,
      143–144
   historical statistics for
      frequently used asset
      classes, 125
   historical statistics for 16 equity
      markets in twentieth
      century, 139
   RMSQ and, 137, 140
   for 16 equity markets in
      twentieth century,
      143–144
Continuous ordering function,
   28–29
Convex utility curve, 12, 13

Covariance
  excess growth and, 79
  for MV, 42
Critical line method, 121
CVaR. *See* Conditional value at risk
CVaR-squared, 137
  for 16 equity markets in twentieth century, 147

Decision makers. *See* Bayesian decision makers; Human decision makers; Rational decision makers
Degrees of freedom, for Student's *t* distributions, 151, 165–166, 190
Density functions, 155–156
  Pearson distributions and, 163
  probability functions and, 157
Dexter, A.S., 70
Dimson, E.P., 77, 80. *See also* DMS database
Discontinuities, 29
DMS database, 137–147, 169–175, 200–201
  annual returns and, 191

EAFE, 80
  geometric mean for, 81
  skew-neutral and, 126
  standard deviation and, 111
EDD, 103
  approximation errors, 89
  HL and, 94
  LMT and, 96
  normal return distributions and, 111
  overestimate with, 102
  underestimate with, 111, 112–113

Ederington, L.H., 63–69
Efficacy of approximation, measurement of, 70
Elements (Euclid), 25
EM, geometric mean for, 81
Emerging markets (EM), 80–81
  standard deviation and, 102
End-of-period EU, 48
Ensemble, 152, 169, 174
  histogram for, 182
  LLH and, 184
  mean for, 183
  near LH-maximizing distributions for, 182–186
  standard deviation for, 183
"The Erroneous Approximation of Expected Utility by Means of a Taylor's Series Expansion: Analytic and Computation Results" (Loistl), 47–48
Estimated variance. *See* Adjusted VaR estimated variance
EU. *See* Expected utility
Euclid, 24, 25
Excess growth, 79
Expected absolute error, 120
Expected mean square error, 120
Expected return
  EU and, 13, 38
  probability distributions and, 42–43
  return distributions and, 91, 150
Expected utility (EU), 1–35
  Allais's paradox and, 17–24
  Axiom III and III' and, 28
  axioms for, 24–31
  bounded versus unbounded utility of returns and, 31–34

220 • Index

Expected utility (EU) (*Cont'd.*)
  call options and, 58
  characteristics of, 12–14
  Ederington, and, 63–69
  end-of-period, 48
  expected return and, 13, 38
  explicit, 41, 43–44, 51, 57
  HDMs and, 18
  implicit, 42, 43–44
  Levy-Markowitz alternative way and, 50
  maximization of, 41–44, 150–151
  mean and, 196
  MV and, 37–72, 77, 169
  MV-approximate, 41, 56
  PB and, 151
  preferences and, 9
  probability distributions and, 196
  quadratic return distributions and, 38
  RDMs and, 29, 150–151
  RDMs versus HDMs, 14–17
  for return distributions, 40
  Taylor-series approximations and, 67
  uniqueness and, 10–12
  variance and, 196
Explicit EU, 41
  implicit EU and, 43–44
  Levy-Markowitz alternative way and, 51
  optimization premiums and, 57
Exponential distributions, 151
Exponential utility function
  call options and, 61
  Levy-Markowitz alternative way and, 53
  MV-approximate EU and, 56
  optimization premiums and, 57
  probability distributions and, 46–47
  quadratic approximation and, 53–54

Fernholz, R., 79
Fishburn, P.C., 30
Flipping coins, 2–3
  lotteries and, 26–28
  probability distributions for, 20

Gamma distributions, 151
Gaussian approximations, 63–69
Generated distributions, 202
Generating distributions, 202
Geometric mean
  adjusted variance and, 129, 132, 133
  approximation errors and, 84–90
  arithmetic mean and, 118
  CVaR and, 135, 143–144
  for EAFE, 81
  for EM, 81
  historical statistics for frequently used asset classes, 125
  historical statistics for 16 equity markets in twentieth century, 139
  MAD and, 128, 141–142
  MV and, 73–121, 138
  nonlinearity of, 78
  Pearson distributions and, 115
  probability distributions and, 33–34, 75
  standard deviation and, 118
  SV and, 128, 141–142
  twentieth-century real equity returns, 97–111

VaR and, 135, 143–144
variance and, 128, 135, 141–144
weighted average of, 79, 118–121
Geometric mean of series, 73–75
Grauer, R.R., 71
Growth rate, 75
inflation and, 197–198

Hakansson, N.H., 70–71
HDMs. *See* Human decision makers
Helms, B.P., 84, 199
Hildreth, C., 151
Histograms, for Pearson distributions, 179–182
HL, 84, 88, 89
absolute error with, 102, 103
approximation errors with, 113
EDD and, 94, 103
LMT and, 96
median estimate with, 100
recommendation for, 114–117
Hlawitschka, W., 58, 61, 62–63
Human decision makers (HDMs)
Allais's paradox and, 28
errors by, 15
EU and, 18
lotteries and, 17
perception by, 15, 30
preferences of, 30
probability distributions and, 15
versus RDMs, 14–17
Weber's Law and, 16–17, 24
Hyperinflation, 80
Hypotheses. *See* Compound hypotheses; Simple hypotheses

Implicit EU, 42
explicit EU and, 43–44
Inflation, 80–82
growth rate and, 197–198
Internal rate of return, 75
Interpolated VaR, 136
historical statistics for frequently used asset classes, 125
return distributions and, 126
variance and, 135

Jean, W.H., 84, 199
Johnson, N.L., 178
Jorion, P., 124

Kahneman, D., 16
Kaplan, P.D., 124
Konno, H., 124
Kontek, K., 16
Weber's Law and, 196
Kroll, Y., 35, 67
Kurtosis
Bayes factors and, 160
lognormal distributions and, 191
Pearson distributions and, 204
of return distributions, 116

Lagrangian, 22
Latané, Henry, 84, 118, 199.
See also HL
Level of return
concave utility curve for, 12, 13
convex utility curve for, 12, 13
outcomes and, 12
strictly concave utility curve for, 12–14
strictly convex utility curve for, 12
utility curves for, 12

Levy, H., 35, 41
  call options and, 61
  Ederington and, 63, 67
  MV and, 169
Levy-Markowitz alternative way
  Ederington and, 66
  MV and, 48–53
Likelihood ratio (LH). *See also*
    Log-likelihood ratio
  AIC and, 202
  Bayes factor and, 156
  belief ratio and, 155
  for Ensemble, 182–186
  mean and, 164–165
  Pearson distributions and,
    156, 163
  standard deviation and,
    164–165
  Student's *t* distributions and,
    165–166, 184–186
Limit approximation (LMT),
    82, 95–97
  approximation errors, 90
  DMS and, 201
  overestimate with, 104
  underestimate of,
    100, 104
LLH. *See* Log-likelihood ratio
LMT. *See* Limit approximation
Logarithmic utility function
  bounded utility function
    and, 34
  choice and, 46
  Levy-Markowitz alternative way
    and, 50
  Loistl and, 48
  MV and, 32, 33–34
  natural, 38–39
  quadratic return distributions
    and, 39

Log-likelihood ratio (LLH), 155
  Bayes factors and, 186
  Ensemble and, 184
  Pearson distributions and, 156,
    163, 203–206
  transformed variables and, 159
Lognormal distributions. *See*
    also Near lognormal
    approximation
  kurtosis and, 191
  skewness and, 191
  transformed variables and, 159
Log-wealth utility function, 196
Loistl, O., 47–48
Lotteries
  Allais's paradox and, 18–20
  flipping coins and, 26–28
  HDMs and, 17
  probability distributions for, 7
  utility and, 22, 196

MAD. *See* Mean absolute
    deviation
MAD-squared, 128, 129. *See also*
    Adjusted MAD-squared
  DMS database and, 140
  for 16 equity markets in
    twentieth century, 145
Markowitz, H.M., 1, 4, 8, 18, 22,
    35. *See also* Levy-Markowitz
    alternative way
  AIC and, 202
  axioms of, 25, 28, 30
  Bayes factors and, 151, 161
  Bayesian decision makers
    and, 190
  call options and, 61
  compound hypotheses
    and, 167
  Ederington and, 63, 67

MV and, 34, 39, 40, 41, 72, 169
Pearson distributions and, 161
quadratic approximation
and, 48, 70
RDMs and, 150–151
transformed variables and,
156–159
Marschak, J., 25
Marsh, P., 80. *See also* DMS
database
Maximum absolute error,
82, 88
Maximum gain, 106
QE and, 108–110
Maximum loss
arithmetic mean and,
104–105
QE and, 108–110
as risk measure, 2–3
by 16 equity markets in
twentieth century, 140
Mean. *See also* Arithmetic mean;
Geometric mean
Ederington and, 66
for Ensemble, 183
EU and, 196
historical statistics for
frequently used asset
classes, 125
historical statistics for 16 equity
markets in twentieth
century, 139
LH and, 164–165
MV and, 42, 75
normal distributions and,
165–166, 198
Pearson distributions and, 204
Student's t distributions and,
165–166
transformed variables and, 158

Mean absolute deviation (MAD),
124. *See also* Adjusted MAD-
squared; MAD-squared
geometric mean and, 128,
141–142
historical statistics for
frequently used asset
classes, 125
historical statistics for 16 equity
markets in twentieth
century, 139
RMSQ and, 129–131
for 16 equity markets in
twentieth century, 141–142
Mean-variance approximations
(MV). *See also*
MV-approximate EU
approximation errors and, 84–90
approximation method
relationships with, 90–97
arithmetic mean and, 77–80
call options and, 58–63
concave utility curve and, 69
Ederington and, 66
efficacy of, 77
EU and, 37–72, 77, 169
geometric mean and, 73–121, 138
inputs for, 42–43, 78–80
Levy-Markowitz alternative way
and, 48–53
logarithmic utility function
and, 32, 33–34
Loistl and, 47–48
method choices for, 111–117
minus-infinite utility and, 39
normal return distributions
and, 150
probability distributions
and, 43
return distributions and, 43

Mean-variance approximations (MV) (Cont'd.)
  risk-aversion and, 53–58
  standard deviation and, 94–95
  symmetric return distributions and, 110
  twentieth-century real equity returns, 97–111
  utility functions and, 77
  utility of return versus utility of wealth and, 44–47
  variance and, 77–78
Menger, K., 32
Minus-infinite utility, 32–33
  MV and, 39
Monte Carlo simulation, 192–193
Monthly returns, 52
  optimization premium and, 56–57
Morgenstern, O., 24–25, 44
Morningstar EnCorr, 80
Mutual funds
  annual returns for, 49, 50, 53
  MV and, 51
MV. *See* Mean-variance approximations
MV-approximate EU, 41
  exponential utility function and, 56

Natural logarithm utility function, 38–39
Near LH-maximizing distributions, for Ensemble, 182–186
Near lognormal approximation (NLN), 83
  approximation errors with, 90, 113
  EDD and, 103
  HL and, 103
  LMT and, 96
  lognormal distributions and, 110, 111
  overestimate of, 100
  recommendation for, 114–117
  return distributions and, 110
  underestimate with, 102
Near-normality approximation, 66–68
NLN. *See* Near lognormal approximation
Normal distributions
  compound hypotheses and, 167
  mean and, 165–166, 198
  practically normal, 175–179
  standard deviation and, 198
Normal probability distributions, 151
Normal return distributions, 38
  EDD and, 111
  MV and, 150
  RVEV and, 133–135

Objective Function, Weber's Law and, 22
One plus return, 197
Optimization premium, 56–57
Ord, K., 162
Outcomes
  axioms and, 32
  certainty and, 195
  level of return and, 12
  preferences for, 195
  probability distributions and, 5–6, 8, 14
  unit utility for, 11
  utility and, 9
  zero utility for, 11
Outliers contribution, 106–108

Paretian distributions, 151–152, 168, 169
Payoffs, Weber's Law and, 16
PB. *See* Probability beliefs
Pearson distributions
　arithmetic mean and, 170–172
　Bayes factors and, 151, 161–169
　compound hypotheses and, 168
　density function and, 163
　geometric mean and, 115
　histograms for, 179–182
　LH and, 156, 163
　LLH and, 156, 163, 203–206
　practically normal distributions and, 175–179
　probability distributions and, 155, 161
　return distributions and, 116
　sample moments for, 188
　skewness and, 163, 189, 204
　standard deviation and, 170–172
　Type I, 170–172, 173, 174
　Type III, 56
　Type IV, 161–162, 163, 170–172, 173, 203–206
　Type VI, 170–172, 173
　Type VII, 162, 163
Perception
　by HDMs, 15, 30
　of preferences, 26, 30
　by RDMs, 15
　Weber's Law and, 196
Posterior beliefs
　Bayes factors and, 154
　Bayes' rule and, 151
Power utility function, 45–46
　choice and, 46
　Levy-Markowitz alternative way and, 50
　probability distributions and, 46

Practically normal distributions, Pearson distributions and, 175–179
Preferences
　Axiom I and, 26
　Axiom II and, 26–27
　Axiom III and III' and, 28
　EU and, 9
　of HDMs, 30
　for outcomes, 195
　perception of, 26
　of RDMs, 9, 26, 28
　utility and, 11
Probability beliefs (PB), 151–152
Probability distributions
　Axiom I and, 25–26
　Axiom II and, 26–27
　Axiom III and III' and, 29
　axioms for, 25–26
　Bayes factors and, 151
　EU and, 196
　expected return and, 42–43
　exponential utility function and, 46–47
　for flipping coins, 20
　geometric mean and, 33–34, 75
　HDMs and, 15
　for lotteries, 7
　MV and, 43
　outcomes and, 5–6, 8, 14
　Pearson distributions and, 155, 161
　power utility function and, 46
　RDMs and, 5, 8–9, 14, 15, 149
　transformed variables and, 158
　utilities and, 10
　vector for, 8
Probability functions, density functions and, 157
Pulley, L.M., 71–72

QE, 104–106
    approximation errors with, 89, 113–114
    DMS and, 201
    EDD and, 103
    HL and, 103
    LMT and, 96
    maximum gain and, 108–110
    maximum loss and, 108–110
    overestimate with, 116
    recommendation for, 114–117
    return distributions and, 110
    underestimate with, 116
Quadratic approximation, 70
    Ederington and, 63–69
    exponential utility function and, 53–54
    Levy-Markowitz alternative way and, 49
    Loistl and, 48
Quadratic return distributions, 38
    logarithmic utility function and, 39
Quiggin, J., 34, 35

Ranking functions, choice by, 30
Rate of return, 197
Rational decision makers (RDMs)
    Allais's paradox and, 28
    axioms for, 25–26
    Bayes factors and, 153
    certainty and, 33
    concave utility curve and, 14
    errors by, 15
    EU and, 29, 150–151
    HDMs versus, 14–17
    perception of, 15
    preferences of, 9, 26, 28
    probability distributions and, 5, 8–9, 14, 15, 149
    unbounded utility of returns and, 33
Raw VaR, 136
    historical statistics for frequently used asset classes, 125
    return distributions and, 126–127
    RVEV and, 135
Raw VaR estimated variance (RVEV), 133–135
RDMs. *See* Rational decision makers
Remote clients, 151
Return. *See also* Expected return; Level of return
    internal rate of, 75
    one plus, 197
    rate of, 197
    single-period utility of, 47
Return distributions, 149–194. *See also* Normal return distributions; Quadratic return distributions; Symmetric return distributions
    EU for, 40
    expected return and, 91, 150
    interpolated VaR and, 126
    kurtosis of, 116
    Levy-Markowitz alternative way and, 49
    likelihood of, 149–194
    MV and, 43
    NLN and, 110
    normal, 38
    Pearson distributions and, 116
    QE and, 110
    quadratic, 38

raw VaR and, 126–127
skewness of, 116
small-cap, 108
standard deviation and, 150
Taylor-series approximations
 and, 111–112
Tessitore, Ansel, and, 149–194
Tessitore, Anthony, and,
 149–194
Usmen, Nilufer, and, 149–194
Risk. *See also* Conditional value at
 risk; Value at risk
alternative measures of,
 123–148
DMS database and, 137–147
maximum loss and, 2–3
measures of, 2–3
standard deviation and, 2–3
Risk-aversion
certainty and, 55
concave utility curve and, 14,
 69, 149, 196–197
MV and, 53–58
risk-free asset and, 56–58
Risk-free asset, 56–58
Root-mean-squared (RMSQ)
adjusted MAD-squared and,
 129–130
CVaR and, 137, 140
DMS database and, 140
MAD and, 129–131
SV and, 140
RVEV. *See* Raw VaR estimated
 variance

Safety-first, 29
Satchell, S., 124
Savage, L.J., 151
Schwartz, G., 202
Semideviation

historical statistics for
 frequently used asset
 classes, 125
historical statistics for 16 equity
 markets in twentieth
 century, 139
SV and, 126
Semi-ex ante simulated returns,
 63–65
Semivariance (SV), 124,
 201. *See also* Adjusted
 semivariance
geometric mean and, 128,
 141–142
RMSQ and, 140
semideviation and, 126
for 16 equity markets in
 twentieth century,
 141–142, 146
symmetric return distributions
 and, 126
variance and, 126
Sharpe-Lintner Capital Asset
 Pricing Model, 71
Shay, B., 79
Simaan, Y., 56–57, 71
Simple hypotheses
Bayes factors and, 160
belief ratio with, 159
Single-period choice situation, 5
Single-period utility of return, 47
Skewness
lognormal distributions and, 191
Pearson distributions and, 163,
 189, 204
of return distributions, 116
Skew-neutral, 126
Small-cap return
 distributions, 108
Sortino, F., 124

Spearman rank correlation coefficients, 58–63
Standard deviation
  approximation errors and, 85–88, 100
  EAFE and, 111
  EM and, 102
  for Ensemble, 183
  geometric mean and, 118
  historical statistics for frequently used asset classes, 125
  historical statistics for 16 equity markets in twentieth century, 139
  LH and, 164–165
  MV and, 94–95
  normal distributions and, 198
  Pearson distributions and, 170–172
  return distributions and, 150
  and risk, 2–3
  transformed variables and, 158
Staunton, M., 80. *See also* DMS database
Step-function probability density, 126
Strictly concave utility curve, 12–14
Strictly convex utility curve, 12
Stuart, A., 162
Student's t distributions, 156, 160
  Cauchy distributions and, 162
  degrees of freedom of, 151, 165–166, 190
  LH and, 165–166, 184–186
  mean and, 165–166
  Pearson Type VII distributions and, 162
  variance and, 168

SV. *See* Semivariance
Symmetric return distributions
  MV and, 110
  SV and, 126

Taylor-series approximations, 58–63, 93
  adjusted variance and, 129
  Ederington and, 66
  EU and, 67
  return distributions and, 111–112
Tessitore, Ansel, 201
  return distributions and, 149–194
Tessitore, Anthony, 201
  return distributions and, 149–194
Transformed variables, 156–159
Trent, R.H., 69–70
Tuttle, D.L., 199
Tversky, A., 16

Unbounded utility of returns, 31–34
  probability distributions and, 32
  RDMs and, 33
Uniform distributions, 126–127, 151
Uniqueness, EU and, 10–12
Unit utility, for outcomes, 11
Usmen, Nilufer, 35, 201
  AIC and, 202
  Bayes factors and, 151, 161
  Bayesian decision makers and, 190
  compound hypotheses and, 167
  Pearson distributions and, 161
  RDMs and, 150–151

return distributions and, 149–194
transformed variables and, 156–159
Utility. *See also* Expected utility
  Bernoulli, 196
  level of return and, 12
  Loistl and, 48
  lotteries and, 22, 196
  minus-infinite, 32–33, 39
  outcomes and, 9
  preferences and, 11
  probability distributions and, 10
  unit, 11
  zero, 11
Utility curves. *See also* Concave utility curve
  convex, 12, 13
  for level of return, 12
  strictly concave, 12–14
  strictly convex, 12
Utility functions. *See also* Exponential utility function; Logarithmic utility function; Power utility function
  bounded, 34
  log-wealth, 196
  MV and, 77
  natural logarithm, 38–39
  VBC and, 68–69
Utility of returns
  bounded, 31–34
  single-period, 47
  unbounded, 31–34
  versus utility of wealth, 44–47
Utility of wealth
  single-period utility of return and, 47
  utility of return versus, 44–47

Value at risk (VaR), 124. *See also* Adjusted VaR estimated variance; Conditional value at risk; Interpolated VaR; Raw VaR; Value at risk
  DMS database and, 140
  geometric mean and, 135, 143–144
  historical statistics for frequently used asset classes, 125
  historical statistics for 16 equity markets in twentieth century, 139
  RVEV, 133–135
  for 16 equity markets in twentieth century, 143–144
Value of blank check (VBC), 55
  utility functions and, 68–69
Van Dijk, E., 35
VaR. *See* Value at risk
Variance. *See also* Adjusted VaR estimated variance; Adjusted variance; Mean-variance approximations
  Bayesian decision makers and, 203
  DMS database and, 140
  Ederington and, 66
  EU and, 196
  geometric mean and, 128, 135, 141–144
  historical statistics for frequently used asset classes, 125
  interpolated VaR and, 135
  MV and, 42, 75, 77–78
  Pearson distributions and, 204
  for 16 equity markets in twentieth century, 141–144, 145
  and Student's *t* distributions, 168
  SV and, 126

VBC. *See* Value of blank check
Vectors, 120, 202
   and probability distributions, 8
Von Neumann, J., 24–25, 44

Wealth
   beginning-of-period, 44, 197
   certainty-equivalent, 70
   end-of-period, 44, 197
   log-wealth utility function, 196
   utility, 44–47
Weber's Law, 15–17, 196
   Allais's paradox and, 21–24
   and extreme cases, 16–17

   HDMs and, 24
   Objective Function
     and, 22
   probability and, 16–17
Weighted average
   of geometric mean, 79
   selection of, 118–121

Yamazaki, H., 124
Young, W.E., 69–70
Yu, J.N.W., 70

Zero utility, for outcomes, 11
Ziemba, W.T., 70

ABOUT THE AUTHORS

Harry M. Markowitz is a Nobel Laureate and the father of Modern Portfolio Theory. Named "Man of the Century" by *Pensions & Investments* magazine, he is a recipient of the prestigious John von Neumann Theory Prize for his work in portfolio theory, sparse matrix techniques, and the SIMSCRIPT programming language.

Kenneth A. Blay serves as a Senior Investment Analyst with 1st Global. He leads asset allocation research and policy recommendations for the firm's investment management platform. He has played an instrumental role in the development of 1st Global's efforts in portfolio management, investment due diligence, capital markets analysis, and the establishment of the Investment Management Research Group, which today oversees all of the firm's portfolio management research efforts. Kenneth has worked extensively with Dr. Harry Markowitz on portfolio analysis, risk management, and various 1st Global research efforts, including tax-cognizant asset allocation.